TO BE A PLAYWRIGHT

TO BE A PLAYWRIGHT

JANET NEIPRIS

Routledge
Taylor & Francis Group
New York   London

Published in 2005 by
Routledge
Taylor & Francis Group
270 Madison Avenue
New York, NY 10016

Published in Great Britain by
Routledge
Taylor & Francis Group
2 Park Square
Milton Park, Abingdon
Oxon OX14 4RN

International Standard Book Number-10: 0-87830-187-9 (Hardcover) 0-87830-188-7 (Softcover)
International Standard Book Number-13: 978-0-87830-187-4 (Hardcover) 978-0-87830-188-1 (Softcover)
Library of Congress Card Number 2005023111

Library of Congress Cataloging-in-Publication Data

Neipris, Janet.
   To be a playwright / by Janet Neipris.
      p. cm.
   Includes bibliographical references and index.
   ISBN 0-87830-187-9 (cloth : acid-free paper) -- ISBN 0-87830-188-7 (pbk. : acid-free paper)
   1. Playwriting. 2. Drama--Technique. I. Title.

PN1661.N45 2005
808.2--dc22
                                                     2005023111

Taylor & Francis Group
is the Academic Division of T&F Informa plc.

Visit the Taylor & Francis Web site at
http://www.taylorandfrancis.com

and the Routledge Web site at
http://www.routledge-ny.com

The copyright information continues on page 241.

This book is dedicated to all my students

Acknowledgments

With thanks to Tina Howe, Barbara Greenberg, Monica Holmes, Liz Diggs, Elizabeth Poliner, Mary Lou Weisman, Richard Rhodes, Mark Ravenhill, Richard Wesley, Len Jenkin, Gary Garrison, Leslie Lee, Norman Levy, Jackie Park, Pari Shirazi, Mark Dickerman, Richard Walter, Israel Horowitz, Myra Appleton, Alonzo Davis, Jim Houghton, Zelda Fischandler, Suzy Graham-Adriani, Kip Gould, Judith Johnson, Bryony Lavery, Shi-Zhen Chen, Victor Lodato, Jackie Jaffee, Gianna Celli, Carol Rocamora, Susan Einhorn, Zach Udko, Zohar Tzur, Rita and Burton Goldberg, Dean David Oppenheim, Dean Mary Schmidt-Campbell, Dean David Finney, Dean Matthew Santirocco, President Emeritus Jay Oliva, Judith Ivey, Freda Foh Shen, Edith Milton, my assistants, Beth Bigler and Portia Krieger, Patricia MacLaughlin, my agent, Cheryl Andrews, my editors, Bill Germano and Frederick Veith, The National Endowment for the Arts, the Rockefeller Foundation, W. Alton Jones Fund, New York University Faculty Research Grant, Virginia Center for the Creative Arts, my daughters Carolyn, Cynthia, and Ellen Neipris, my husband, Donald Wille, and those I hold in memory, who believed in me — Elliot Norton, Stuart Browne, Venable Herndon, Larry Marcus, Charlie Purpura, Lois Gould, Debra James, and Eve Merriam.

Contents

Introduction

The house where I grew up was in a neighborhood of miles of three-decker wooden houses with front and back porches, cellar doors, and postage-stamp yards and back alleys, where kids called out "Alley, alley entrée" across fences. We lived in a house next to the lady who sold gravestones, Mrs. Galarnaux. Once a year, on Memorial Day, with four cemeteries at the end of the street, our neighborhood became the center of that time and place where I grew up. Early in the morning, the bands would form at the corner, shining their instruments and warming up while Mrs. Galarnaux would set out wreaths and flower baskets of red geraniums, and her two sons would dust off the monument displays, eager for passersby on their way to decorate the graves of their loved ones.

At the same time, the soldiers would assemble — the American Legion, the Veterans of Foreign Wars, the Jewish War Veterans (led for many years by my father who was the president of the Herbert J. Woolf Post), then the Sons of Italy, followed by the Boy Scouts, the band from St. Angela's Catholic Church, the Fire Department, and anyone who had someone buried at the end of that street, which was practically everyone — women and children and soldiers and policemen and dogs, all preparing to step to the tune of John Philip Sousa. Those were patriotic days, on the wings of World War II.

Our neighborhood was populated by immigrants, the newly arrived Irish, Jewish, and Italian families, all eager to Americanize their children. And, for these families, the path to paradise was education. It's not surprising, therefore, that this Mattapan-Dorchester-Roxbury area spawned the likes of Leonard Bernstein, Theodore White, actor Leonard Nimoy (his father owned the barber shop next door to the shoe store where my father worked as a salesman), college presidents, Nobel Prize winners, heads of corporations, leading scientists, lawyers, architects, politicians, professors, and countless artists and writers. We were encouraged to have dreams and ride those dreams straight out of the neighborhood and into the wide world. Most of us were given permission to inhabit worlds larger than our parents'.

In the popular movies of the day, Dick Haymes and Fred Astaire were songwriters, knocking on doors and selling tunes the world had been waiting for, like "My Blue Heaven." In these films the characters would get rich, get the girl, lose the girl, and after moderate anguish, win back the girl, vowing never to let her go. They played pianos, made music, and how I longed to be like them, creating songs and stories, as I sat there under the make-believe stars of the Oriental Theatre on a Saturday afternoon.

The opening of the Mattapan Free Library, on the very next street to ours, was a major event. The walls were stacked with thousands of volumes, and true to its name, they were free. In those days of limited means, "free" was a magic word. The Children's Room of the library had a dozen round wooden tables and small chairs, and all of it brand new. In a world where we were crowded into railroad apartments, and privacy was virtually unknown, here was a place you could go and enter your own space.

My initiation to the library was the Story Hour, held every Saturday, and thankfully, after my favorite children's radio show

Let's Pretend had broadcast. At the appointed time, the librarian would sit on a chair and we would encircle her on the floor. She would read two stories, holding up the illustrations, page by page. At the end of the stories, the child who could guess the number closest to the one she was thinking of could check out the books for two weeks. It never occurred to any of us children to question her integrity. If she said she had been thinking of nine and you guessed nine, you were victorious. It was very prestigious to get those books all to yourself and under the covers of your bed.

Once I could read, my favorite section of the library was biographies. I raced through the lives of composers — Mozart, Beethoven, Hadyn, Mendelssohn. I dreamed of being like them and creating music. Once I entered junior high school, like all girls my age, I read the Sue Barton nurse stories; however, I was much more taken by the series about a woman journalist named Peggy. There was *Peggy Covers Washington*, *Peggy Covers London*, and just plain *Peggy Covers the News*. When I look back to those days, I realize the beginnings of the dream of being a writer and composer were being hatched.

At home, we had only three books: one belonged to my father, the other to my mother, and the third was the sacred family volume of poems. My father had a copy of Aldous Huxley's *Point Counter Point*. I have no idea how he came to the book, and my mother claimed he had never even read it, but he proclaimed it to be his favorite book of all time. It was bright red and kept behind glass cabinet doors in my parent's bedroom. My mother's book was a small, brown, leather-bound volume of *The Rubiyat of Omar Khayam*, and it was inscribed with one of the verses:

> To my darling,
> "And the night shall be filled with music
> And the cares that infect the day
> Shall fold their tents like the Arabs
> And silently steal away."

The pages were lined with gold, and my mother kept it hidden in a bureau drawer. I never found out exactly who the giver was, but my mother once told me it was the man she should have married, and that he took her to concerts and the theatre and introduced her to poetry. The third book was oblong and brown, with a paper cover. *One Hundred and One Famous Poems* had the photo of each poet, in an oval at the top of every page, and there wasn't a poem in the book I hadn't memorized by the time I entered high school. All the old favorites were there, from Wordsworth's "Daffodils" to Whitman's "Captain My Captain," and Longfellow's "Children's Hour" to Rudyard Kipling's "Gunga Din." I was particularly interested in the women poets, Emily Dickinson, Edna St. Vincent Millay, Elizabeth Barrett Browning, and George Eliot. It's interesting that when I later became literary editor of the high school yearbook for Roxbury Memorial High School for Girls, in my senior year, I decided to find a quote for every graduating woman, and found all the quotes I needed in this one book.

I never set out to be a writer. My family's aspirations for me were more in the traditional line of secretarial work. When I applied and gained acceptance to Boston Girls Latin School, a prestigious and vigorous public high school for young women who planned on attending college, I was discouraged from attending. It was foolish to dream of something that couldn't be. And that is how I found myself at Roxbury Memorial High School for Girls, in the commercial track, with an emphasis on typing, bookkeeping, sewing, and childcare.

But writing evidences itself at a young age, for most, and comes out of the desire to tell a story.

The first show I ever wrote was an adaptation of *Little Women*, with me playing all the parts. The presentation was on my front porch, and I paid the neighborhood children twenty-five cents apiece out of my baby-sitting money to persuade them to attend.

Then Miss Sophia Palm came into my life. She was my English teacher in junior year, and she believed in celebrating Shakespeare's birthday every April with daffodils. She encouraged original writing. Although she taught both the college and the commercial tracks, her requirements for each class were the same — ten original short stories, twenty original poems, and twenty books to be read, and all of them classics. She took the education of the mind seriously.

After I wrote my first short story for Miss Palm, she called me in after school and asked what I was doing in a commercial track when I had promise as a writer and should be preparing to go to college. When she learned of my family's circumstances, which were as much economic as societal, she asked to see my parents. To be honest, I don't remember whether they ever met with Miss Palm, but that summer, under her guidance, I attended summer school, taking every necessary college course in science, math, and languages required to take the SAT and the College Boards and apply to colleges. Nights and weekends I managed to keep my job as a bookkeeper at a local hospital mainly to satisfy my parents.

For every writer, there is always the story of that teacher who encouraged the talent, and that certainly entered into my present commitment to education. For years Miss Sophia Palm and I corresponded at Christmas time. The year that no card arrived, I knew she had died. But she was the inspiration and the reason for my turn in the road at that time.

Because I had been in the commercial track, I had also missed out on much of the drilling that went on in preparation for taking college entrance exams; so I dated only boys who were at Boys Latin School and had spent the last two years learning the necessary drills in order to compete well in the exams. These were neighborhood boys who had their sights to Harvard. They were only too happy to share their preparatory expertise with me. Saturday nights were devoted to synonyms, antonyms, and multiple-choice questions.

I was accepted at Tufts University the next spring, and with full scholarship and added aid from the Women's Scholarship Association in Boston, I started my college career as a commuter. Most of the students at Tufts were residential at that time, and so, to be a commuter was a lowly thing. But no matter, I would major in English literature and philosophy and attempt to read every book in the college library. The only actual writing course I took at Tufts was one given by John Holmes, the poet, who also told me I would be a writer one day. But, at the same time, I was working twenty hours a week at the hospital and receiving a great deal of pressure from my family to help out even more than I had been. In those years my father was beset by heart problems and was in and out of hospitals and work. When my father, whom I adored, died at the end of my freshman year, it felt like the bottom had fallen out of my world. It seemed doubtful that I would even return for my sophomore year of college. My financial and emotional help was needed at home.

The previous spring, in the Tufts Chapel, I had heard Robert Frost read aloud his poem "The Road Not Taken" and somehow knew this was the moment of decision for me. If I stayed home, I would never get out of this place. My only chance to have a life different from my mother's was to go back to college — but without family approval. It was then that the Women's Scholarship Association came through giving me enough money to live away at school.

I moved into the dormitories at Tufts on public transportation with one suitcase, as all the shiny cars filled with parents and students and "stuff" were pulling into College Row in Medford, Massachusetts.

I had assured my family I would give them half the money earned weekends at the hospital, but to no avail. Every night I put my money in the telephone slot in our dorm, called my mother, and every night, for a long time, she hung up.

But what does this have to do with writing? A lot. The perseverance, discipline, and self-reliance in the face of the rejection, which I lived through in those days, proved excellent preparation for the warrior life demanded of all writers.

In the 1950s, no matter your talent, marriage was on your minds, and so, marry I did, before my senior year. By graduation I was pregnant, and the rest is a hop, skip, and jump across a dozen years of raising three girls.

At the time it seemed natural to help the elementary schools my daughters attended with writing children's shows (I was not as good at baking cookies) for holiday presentations. The first show I actually wrote was for the Boston Parks Department, and it was about a dragon. An artist friend made the puppets, and the show toured all the playgrounds in Boston, with our children working the puppets. The major scene involved a snowstorm, and my daughters, standing on high chairs, sprinkled Ivory Snow Soap all over the stage. I also wrote a show for Lincoln's Birthday called *The Folks at Pigeon Creek*, and one year I adapted *Little Women* for the elementary school, composing original music.

My children were already teenagers when the Women's Scholarship Association came into my life again. I had been doing some volunteer work for them, making some fund-raising speeches as a former "scholarship girl," when they asked if I could possibly write a show for their fiftieth anniversary, celebrating their work in women's education. They had remembered that I had been "kind of a writer in college."

So, I stepped up to the bat, did the research for the musical at Radcliff's Schlessinger Library, used a friend's piano to compose the music, and *A Time to Remember*, based on the history of women in education, was presented at the Statler Hilton Hotel in Boston in the spring of 1967.

In the audience that day was the distinguished Boston theatre critic Elliot Norton. He was to give a speech on the American theatre following the presentation of the musical. Elliot Norton was a gentle giant of a man whose fierce patrician speech and elegant carriage belied the gentleness underneath. He was one of the most respected critics in the country, having recently died at the age of one hundred.

At the close of that afternoon, Mr. Norton approached me, informing me that I was expected at his offices at Boston University the following day. Mr. Norton was not one to dillydally. At the time he was an adjunct instructor of playwriting at the university. He wanted to take me on as a student. When I explained I did not have the necessary funds to do graduate work, he brushed it aside. There were to be no charges. He was certain I had talent. I wasn't. But whatever it was, he wanted to encourage it.

Under his tutelage I wrote my first serious play, *Rousing Up the Rats Again*, based on the twenty-fifth reunion of a group of Holocaust survivors. Its title came from the last paragraph of Albert Camus's novel *The Plague*: "Joy is always imperiled: the plague bacillus never dies or disappears for good; it can lie dormant for years. The day would come when it would rouse up its rats again and send them forth to die in a happy city."

Elliot Norton was a taskmaster, and when after the first draft I was ready to submit it, he sternly admonished that this was only the beginning. I was too eager to give up "my child." Six rewrites later, I had a decent play, and with that draft, at the age of thirty-eight, now with three teenage daughters, I applied to Brandeis University's theatre program as a playwright. You must know that I did not expect to be accepted. They accepted only three playwrights per year. With what I thought was little hope, I thought about taking education courses and teaching high school English. That same spring I was accepted at Brandeis.

Somewhere in those years I collaborated with my friend Barbara Greenberg on a children's musical based on a story she had written. It was called *Jeremy and the Thinking Machine*, and it ran for almost six months at the Thirteenth Street Theatre in New York. When I later went on to serious studies, *Jeremy* was lying in wait in a trunk. Like the plague bacillus, and like all plays, it remained dormant until 2003. Then, through an odd set of circumstances, it was discovered by the National Theatre in London and opened there, as part of the "Connections" program for young audiences, in the summer of 2004.

The two years at Brandeis were intense, between studying, writing, trying to catch up on everything I did not know about the theatre, and at the same time, raising three teenaged girls. I was also married to a doctor, and the social obligations connected to his position were numerous. If it was the theatre that was partially responsible for our eventual separation, it was also my liberation, and only in those years did I begin to feel I was in the right life. Israel Horowitz was my playwriting teacher, and it was from him I learned almost everything there was to know about the theatre. He had this old VW red bus, and he would drive all the students around in it on excursions to everything from theatre performances to Chinese food. We were connected. We were a team. He even convinced the entire class to come to New York a few times, and if I remember correctly, we must have stayed with him on West 12th Street. Israel was also responsible for setting up a New York production for all the Brandeis playwrights at the Cubiculo Theatre. And we even got a review, and if memory serves me, an excellent one.

In addition to his model as teacher, Israel had three children and was a single parent with shared custody (and this was pre-*Kramer vs. Kramer*). Sometimes we would team up with all our kids and go out in the VW bus. We would stop to buy sneakers or bread or go to a bookstore because one of the children needed a certain book for school, and this would be combined with some theatre business, like seeing a show or a producer, or we would meet one of Israel's theater pals visiting from Paris or Belgium.

In this way, Israel served as the only model I had of a playwright who also had family responsibilities. It was what made me certain I could write a play and go to the supermarket all on the same day. Up to then I had a rarified image of playwrights, akin to Lillian Hellman, living hard on the beaches of Martha's Vineyard and Malibu. It was a man who gave me the courage to live my life as a playwright and a woman, and for that, I am eternally grateful.

The love affair with the theater and with playwriting was on its way. On graduation, Israel Horowitz sent for me from the Goodman Theatre in Chicago. At the time, one of his Wakefield plays was in production on the main stage. Well, it seems the Goodman had a second stage, and they had just lost a production. Israel suggested two of the one-act plays I had written in his class — *Statues* and *The Bridge at Belharbour*. Within days, I was on a plane to Chicago where I would work with director Gregory Mosher, and meet the actress who was to star in my plays, then in one of her first professional productions — Judith Ivey. The rest, as they say, is history. And the best thing I can say is that I persevered, and it has certainly been worth it.

The career as an educator began the year of my graduation from Brandeis. Goddard College in Vermont was beginning a correspondence program in writing. The students and faculty would meet twice a year, in summer and winter for two weeks on the campus of Goddard in Vermont. The rest of the year the professors would receive the students' work by mail, comment on it, and send it back. It was my early collaborator Barbara Greenberg, who had been hired as a poet, who called to say Goddard was looking for a playwriting teacher. So I signed on.

The Goddard program, at the time, was legendary. The writing professors were all at the beginning of their careers, and the program was run by poet Ellen Bryan Voight. The faculty included John Irving, Richard Ford, Richard Rhodes, Donald Hall, George Chambers, Louise Gluck, Michael Ryan, Raymond Carver, Tess

Gallagher, Craig Nova, Rosellen Brown, Bob Haas, Steve Dobbins, and more. In that program were some of the legendary writers of the last quarter of the twentieth century. And it all was happening in the midst of the Vietnam years.

After Goddard, and in the middle of a divorce, the economic challenges of living as a playwright were becoming insurmountable, despite productions at some major venues and some television writing. With two daughters in college, Bowdoin and Tufts, and no help with their tuition, I was desperate. The head of the English Department at Tufts was a neighbor, and I had met him once at a party. So, I bicycled over to his house, a few blocks away. It was mid-August, and he had just lost one of his teachers, and he hired me, right there in his backyard.

My daughters immediately set themselves the task of reviewing basic grammar with me. Grammar was not one of my strong suits. I then went on to teach at Harvard and at Tufts for three years. What's more, I was good at teaching and I adored it. When New York University was looking for an adjunct in their newly formed dramatic writing program at the School of the Arts, I was hired, and I moved to New York, together with my second husband, Donald. Now I could be an authentic writer, live in the Village, do some teaching, and never have to wear a little black dress with pearls again!

When I was asked the following year to be interim chair, I wasn't fearful of the duties, but more of the administrative burden, which would no doubt affect my writing time. But it was only for a semester. And also, I was determined to continue writing plays and to debunk the myth that you could not teach and write at the same time. My years in training as a mother ensured the ability to multitask and to focus in a compartmentalized way.

No one was more surprised or elated when, after a long search for a new chair, they asked me to head the department. David Oppenheim, then dean of the newly titled Tisch School of the

Arts, invited me to lunch. My husband claimed that no one ever invites you to lunch in order to tell you that you did *not* get something. The job was mine. I remember to this day ordering fruit salad and never taking one bite, so Dean Oppenheim still owes me a proper lunch!

You see, I loved the shaping of a curriculum, the hiring of a faculty, the admissions process, the building of a theater, and all the possibilities ahead for this very new department of dramatic writers. I saw that as chair you were able to affect change. Also, I was convinced that the education of dramatic writers depended on only three things — the faculty, the curriculum, and the students — in other words, who was doing the teaching, what they were teaching, and whom they were teaching.

Eighteen years later, a major department of dramatic writing had been forged. Our faculty was among the most active playwrights and screenwriters in the country, our diverse student body was recruited from every ethnic pocket there was, and our curriculum consisted of a broad scope of courses that would ensure the education of literate, crafted, and first-rate playwrights and screenwriters.

Some of our alumnae came to include George Woolf, Ken Lonergan, Neil LaBute, Chris Shinn, Phyllis Naige, Heather McDonald, Doug Wright, Frank Pugliese, Jessica Goldberg, Neena Beeber, Producer Susan Cantsonis, Stan Seidel, John Fusco, Daniel Goldfarb, and John Beluso.

As an educator, I never stopped teaching what I knew to the next generation, and as a writer, I never stopped writing. My husband, Donald, an engineer and a sculptor, told me recently that I finally got the life I deserved. What I did get was the life I always wanted — to be in Greenwich Village, to write, to teach, and to live.

1

THE TWELVE HABITS OF SUCCESSFUL PLAYWRIGHTS

For me, the stage will always be a place where large things happen. Most plays are about unique individuals coming together in moments of crisis, which lead to conflicts, which lead to confrontations, which lead to resolutions, and finally to change.

Plays are a process. They are subject to human error as well as spontaneous magnificence. They are acted out by people who have daily lives, whose cars break down, whose children break down, and whose dogs run away. They are supported by a stage manager, lighting, set, sound, and costume designers, as well as a director, all subject to the same dailyness. Plays are attended by live audiences who change from night to night, according to the weather, time of day, and their own lives. If you ever doubted that each audience as a collective has its own personality, sit through the run of a play and see the transformation of the play every night.

There is an aliveness in plays because they celebrate the dynamic of the moment, not telling about "how" it happened, but rather being there as the event occurs, as the characters come to a kind of realization, the "a-ha moment." You are writing about people putting themselves on the line, in most instances, with no moonlit hills to hide behind, except metaphorical ones. On any ordinary day, when placing two unique individuals together, anything is possible.

In creating the world of a play, we are filling a space that formerly went unused in the universe. For the playwright, the world of ideas corresponds to the heavens. We sleep under the light of stars, the light of stars that have long since ceased to exist, and we pattern the actions of our characters on a reality which we create and which ceases to exist outside the text and its performance. Our work lives in the theater, by its rules and by its whims. Early on, as playwrights, we learn that the law of certainty is not certain at all. Yes, if we toss a coin in the air, 50 percent of the time it will fall on heads and 50 percent of the time on tails, but only if we toss the coin into infinity. In our lifetime we will not see this law of averages play itself out.

A win is not promised as a playwright. The best we can do is practice habits that do not guarantee success but auger well for it. We do the best we can in an uncertain world. We run down the center of the road well armed, understanding that the slings and arrows of both good fortune and unfortunate fortune will hit us; what we don't do is hide in the bushes where nothing has the chance of hitting us. The playwright is out on the road. The playwright endures by being a warrior and sustaining a financial reality. The days of the starving artist in the garret are over.

As an educator of thousands of playwrights, as well as witness to my colleagues in the theater and on the Dramatists Guild Council, I have observed those habits that appear to be common to successful playwrights. If Freud was correct that love and work are the cornerstones of our humanness[1] then success is becoming the best of whom we are and locating and embracing our uniqueness.

In all the years of teaching I have never encountered the same voice twice — dozens of love stories, countless efforts of characters to escape their beginnings, hundreds of mis-steps which lead to an excess of misfortune, numerous Oedipus-like stories where we watch the hero ride the waves naively to his or her own destruction. Not one voice is like another. So hold to your voice and only write what no one else could write but you.

Preliminary observations in a day of a successful playwright:

1. Get up
2. Make a pot of coffee
3. Sharpen pencils
4. Feed your animal. If you don't have an animal, buy one
5. Forage for food in the fridge
6. Consider writing something
7. You are out of bread. Go to the market
8. Gas up the car while you're out. You are only on half full
9. Call your mother. It's her birthday
10. Vow to start writing
11. Turn on the computer
12. Check the e-mail

Stop. It's lunchtime. Meet a friend for lunch and complain about the state of the theater... a typical day? Sometimes. But let's begin again. New day.

Writing for the theater is a moral as well as an intellectual challenge. How we act, not what we say, fashions our identity as serious writers for the theater. In other words, the playwright is simply one who writes plays, one who piles up the pages. That is the true fabric of our being. Someone can say all they want that "I am a playwright," but as we know, character is action, and we, as the creators, know the truth of our dailyness. Our success as playwrights lies in the deep habits of that dailyness — the unalienable truth when we get into bed in the deep of the night — who we truly are, how we really live our lives, not how we say we do.

So, the twelve habits of highly successful playwrights:

1. Focus

Focus infers a clear vision of the play you are writing, a centering and entering process — going for the very heart of the question you are asking in the play. We write, as Joan Didion said, to discover what it is we are writing about. It's helpful to understand the generating moment for our plays, because we want to keep coming back to it like a homing pigeon. It delivers the roots of the work and so gives us clues and reminds us of the focus.

You begin writing with an amorphous oozing ball in your hands. You then take a bat to it and hit it again and again until it becomes harder and smaller and you can hold the essence of your play in one hand. Call it theme, call it spine, but focus your attention on it. I often write the focus of my play, once I get it, on a card and hang it above my computer. Also above the computer is a permanent index card reading "No one asked you to be a Playwright."

The index card for my current project reads, "The Necessity of Forgiveness." The previous project was "A Gift Is Only a Gift if Someone Can Afford to Accept It." By keeping the center of the play clearly in sight, the playwright tries to hold to the line and spine of the play and not take side trips into the lush countryside. No play can be about the entire world.

So, find the focus and stay there. Find the question you are positing with each play. The following are some of the questions I have asked in my plays:

- Should we forgive violent actions?
- Should the victim forgive the perpetrator?
- What is the nature of evil?
- Can you impose love?
- How far will we go in the name of friendship when our private desires are called into play?
- Where is the separation between parent and child?
- How can you know a country simply by studying its history?

Focus also means keeping to a writing schedule. Mark it out in your calendar. It doesn't matter what time of day, or how long, or where. I know one writer who writes one page a day. That's his rule. If he exceeds his expectations, that's a spectacular day. This writer completes at least 365 pages a year. In a good year he writes two projects or one project with six rewrites. But he is regular and keeps to his schedule.

2. Passion

Passion is what sustains perseverance. You must believe that the play you are writing must be written. The same as you have to know what your characters will fight for and how far they will go, you have to believe you would go to the mat for this play, like a parent for a child. You have to believe that you are the only one in the world who could tell the story. Write from your greatest strength and your joy.

I once began to write a play at the suggestion of an artistic director of a regional theater. The subject — the life and loves of an eminent American playwright, Lillian Hellman, and her life with Dashiel Hammett — was fascinating, with opportunities for research into the personal life of this writer through her letters and interviews. The subject had never yet been done and was eminently commercial. It would be hard to believe this project would not excite any living playwright.

I received the rights to the material and began. But the more research I did and the more I learned, the less I was in love with the subject. It remained a great idea, but not for me. The director who had suggested the subject called to ask, "Do you hear the play singing yet?" "No" I replied, "but that will come." Well, it never did. So after six months of work, with many scenes outlined and written but no fire from inside, I abandoned the project and never looked back.

Someone else eventually wrote that play, but I was grateful it wasn't me. Write from the heart. Believe in the fire. It's what delivers the work. It keeps you honest. Passion comes from our strongest beliefs and questions, those things in our society which anger us, those patterns of human behavior that betray the soul out of greed, jealousy, sheer opportunism, and ambition. Passion requires conviction and conviction demands a moral stance. Know what you stand for and have your characters do battle in its name.

3. A Clear Understanding of the Process

Playwrights who are successful understand that our careers have topography. Only when we have come to the end of our days can we see the shape of a whole career, how it adds up. And this is the thing — it all counts, but the shape of each of our playwriting paths differs as much as the shape of our bodies.

I had an occasion recently to name three alumnae awards at New York University. When I identified one playwright for the award, she was shocked. "You don't want me," she said. "I'm not famous like the others who are getting the awards. I just have this tiny stuff done in teensy theaters no one ever heard of." But she was wrong. She had maintained a constant presence in small experimental theaters across the country. She was working in the theater and ten readings finally did lead to a production in New York. Trust the process of your own path and don't look to anyone else's pattern.

Having a clear understanding of the process also means the craft. We are always lost. As writers our job is to be lost. We start out knowing nothing but the glimmer of an idea. The world of one play cannot prepare us for the world of the next. We are always explorers, breaking fresh ground, and there are no certain answers.

Expect to be lost until you find your way and then lose it once again. At the same time, do not mythologize craft. There are governing rules of theater that are common to all good drama: a character has to be in a different place at the end of the play than at the beginning, obstacles have to escalate, one scene must push the next scene forward, and so forth. Think of yourself as a shoemaker making a pair of shoes, each one different, but all constructed of the best materials, sewn firmly, each one an original, each one with the mark of the craftsman.

4. Perseverance

The race does not always belong to the swiftest or the most talented. Nothing is as heartbreaking as to watch a writer of medium talent persevere, believe in him- or herself above everything, and subsequently outrun the more talented writer who does not have the stamina to stay in the race.

Make no mistake. This is not a race to win, but a race to stay true to yourself and your vision. If you decide writing for the theater is not for you, then stop and become what you really want.

But if you want to be a writer, there will not be a cheerleader at your back. Be determined to write the best you can and about something that catches your passion, and then do battle.

5. Living as a Warrior

As a writer, you are going into battle every day. Therefore, you have to live as though you are in training. Get enough sleep. Exercise. Eat healthy. Don't lead a social life that is killing you, and as one warrior writer friend wisely stated "Don't piss it away on lunch." If you believe in the connectedness of mind and body, this is a purely intellectual profession that requires physical stamina and clarity. Preserve your energy for your work. Don't squander it away. Save the best of yourself for your work. The legend of the dissipated writer is much overrated.

6. Rewriting as Opportunity

The most experienced writers see rewriting as a possibility to make the script better, to throw away their darlings, to edit, to make it lean and mean, to pin emotional moments down to paper like a butterfly, and to make every line integral to the character or the plot.

We have to learn to listen and hear the fat and cut it out, to hear the missing beat and write it in. "We must," as one theater critic told me at the beginning of my career, "want to hold on to our plays as a mother would a child. Oh let me have it just for a while longer and I will make it better." Remember, you are batting around that oozing ball until it is hard as truth.

7. Take on Large Themes and Paint a Complex Canvas

The best theater is hard work for audiences, but it rewards by making them rise to its challenge. If we want to raise the stature of theater, we must tackle complicated and difficult subjects. Effort is precisely what many of us have been avoiding in the theater. It requires us as playwrights to make clear works of art about complex subjects. We live in a universe that often eludes meaning, and it is the writers who have to question it. If not the artist, than who?

8. Emotional Verity

A writer recently presented this problem: I know how to plot and how to write dialogue but how do I write emotion so the characters are believable? The answer is simple. The playwright must be schizophrenic. You must become each character emotionally as he or she speaks. You must change your persona with every speech. That's a lot of twisting and turning; but verity depends on this individuation and also the taking on by the playwright of the emotional substructure of the scene.

If it is a scene about humiliation, we have to go back to those moments when we were actually humiliated. And if the scene is about falling in love, then it requires going back to that moment of rapture, or the moment, if called for, of rage or betrayal or utter disappointment or rejection by pinning the emotion to a piece of our own emotional past.

9. Ever the Professional

Rejection is not personal. I know it feels that way, but it is a matter of someone wanting what you have to sell. It takes only one producer to like your work and many to turn you down, the same as falling in love. If not we would have hundreds of proposals. You don't work with a director or a designer because they are your friends. This is always a matter of who is best for your work. It is always a case of the work. Concentrate on giving your work the best life — the life it deserves.

10. Imposing the Plot

Plot is not a matter of artistic enlightenment. Do not wait for the muses for your plot. Plot is simply mechanical. It is a means of testing the characters, causing them to change, heightening the drama, and keeping things moving. Plot has nothing to do with art and everything to do with escalating obstacles. First this happened, which leads to this happening, which leads to the next happening, and then the moment of highest action, after which everything is changed and there is no going back.

If you don't want to deal with plot, write poetry and talk about the moonlight coming through the trees. And if you want to take your time with the action and stop along the way to watch the sunset spreading over the hills of San Clemente, write a novel. In a play there is no time to stop — keep on pushing. You are on the road.

11. Aggressive Marketing

Be aggressive with marketing your work — and marketing it is, agent or not. No one will take care of your work as much as you will. Yes, an agent will do it, but you are not their only client. Your agent may be enthusiastic, your friends may or may not be supportive, and your mother may pledge her undying belief in you, but the thing that matters in the dark of the night is you and your own belief that someone out there will want your work.

As it turns out, the life of a play is very long and it may flow and ebb. The play may appear in California, be quiet for a while like a hibernating bear, then wake up in Kentucky, then go to sleep again and turn up in New Jersey. For example, everyone says after those New Jersey reviews, it is going straight to New York, but it goes instead to Cincinnati, and then shows up in Singapore only to come back to New York via Munich — and then who knows. The life of the play is forever and no one can predict its full path.

Also, never apologize for calling or writing a theater to inquire about your script. Theaters are in the business of producing playwrights, and you are whom they need. You are their best clients. They are there to produce your work after all. Gear yourself up, make the call for example, — "Hello, this is Edward Albee and I was just inquiring as to the whereabouts of the play I sent you about the baby." Go forth and conquer.

12. And Finally . . .

1. Get up
2. Make a pot of coffee
3. Feed your animal. If you don't have one, buy one. And so forth.

In other words, live a totally evolved life: read, have friends, go out for dinner, go to the gym, go on a trip, drive to the store, meditate, levitate, celebrate. Be totally engaged in life, which is our material, our landscape, our feeding ground, our nourishment, and our teacher.

Conclusion

Focus, passion, a clear understanding of process, perseverance, living as a warrior, rewriting as opportunity, tackling complex themes and growing in your reach, emotional verity, professionalism, imposing the plot, aggressive marketing, and total engagement in life: these are the things that make a successful playwright.

Nothing is guaranteed — not health or wealth, not beauty or power, not the Pulitzer Prize, or the Academy Award — but honor and grace are choices in each of our lives. Being who we say we are gives us the best opportunity to be a success, to become what we want to be, and to embrace what we accomplish in our lifetime.

This lecture was delivered to the members of the Dramatist's Guild of America in Los Angeles California, February 2001. It has been slightly revised for inclusion in this book.

Three Exercises in the Twelve Habits

1. Post an index card in your workspace stating the focus of the play you are currently working on.

2. In a notebook list two possible future projects that take on larger themes than you are currently working on.

3. Make three calls today to literary managers telling them you are a playwright, you have a new play, and describing in one sentence what the play is about. Ask if you may send them the play. If they say "yes," send the plays out within the next two days.

2

A ROOM OF YOUR OWN

To be a writer means you have a space you keep sacred for your work. I know one playwright who works at a small corner of her dining room, at a desk facing the Hudson River, index cards neatly printed, taped to the window above. I know another who writes only in the office at the university where he teaches. The room is windowless, but plastered with circus posters and funky signs proclaiming "Eat at Joe's, the best barbecue in Texas." Usually some country music is playing behind the closed doors (open only during office hours). The place is a mess, papers and books strewn everywhere, stale cigars in ashtrays. How does he find anything in there? He is a brilliant playwright, always experimental and unique, always working, and who has a huge following. But don't dare disturb anything on his desk, because he knows where everything is. Another playwright I know lives with his partner, also a dramatic writer, in a house they designed in upstate New York. There are two writer's rooms, built and furnished like identical twins, on either side of the second floor. They are mirror images. Everything is sleek and shiny. Every piece of paper is out of sight, hidden in some wonderful pull out drawer in the recesses of the wall. The place is seamless. It looks as though no one works here — but they do. Both playwrights are always juggling three or four projects — planning, rewriting, editing. They are serious and their output is prodigious. They simply value and need order. This workplace works for them. They could not accomplish what they do amid the chaos of the described university office. Another playwriting colleague works in a warehouse loft. There is only one thing hanging on his wall — a painting of an old Royal typewriter. Oh what I would do to own that painting—or maybe I wouldn't. It is a *very large* typewriter, after all, and there is something demanding about its imposing image. Maybe I wouldn't want that much guilt staring at me all day.

We all have sacred spaces and amulets to match. On top of our computers you will find precious stones or strange powders or eyes of newt. Whatever does it.

Virginia Woolf in *A Room of One's Own* is speaking in response to the centuries of women who were "locked out" of "writing rooms" because of sociological and economic pressures. By "locked out," Woolf is referring to both the writing professions and the actual physical writer's room. Until the nineteenth century, it was rare for a woman to have a quiet room of her own or professional ambitions. Jane Austen, for example, hid her manuscripts, or covered them with a piece of blotting paper. Louisa May Alcott's Jo in *Little Women* hid in the attic to do her writing. Women were long confined to "making puddings, knitting stockings, playing the piano, and embroidering bags[1]," says Woolf.

But women are not alone in being "locked out" of their rooms. Even in the twenty-first century, there are still those who are denied entrance into certain rooms, either because of ethnicity, economics, social status, or gender. Then, there are those of us who deny ourselves the benefit of a place, usually because of questions of entitlement — we don't think we deserve a room of our own.

In New York City, a group of writers banded together, rented a space, and formed the Writer's Room designed with cubicles, a common space, and funded with small donations and minimal rental fees. Admission is by application. This model for artists is duplicated in cities throughout the world.

Then there is the writer's room away from home — the colony studio. In writer's colonies, for example, from McDowell, Yaddo, and Virginia Center for the Creative Arts in the United States, to the Rockefeller Foundation's Serbelloni Villa in Bellagio, Italy and the Camargue Foundation in France, writers can apply for residencies that furnish them with room and board in addition to a writing studio. Writer's residencies worldwide are listed in publications such as *Grants and Awards for American Writers*, published by PEN, as well as corresponding publications for individual countries.

For those of us who have chosen to be artists, and who enjoy that privilege, a room of our own where we can create what we wish is imperative. Each of us in our own way, as singular as our writers' voices, make a home of our writer's space. It is that place, as Robert Frost says, that lets us in when we come to the door. We are ensured safety.

Recently, at an artists' colony in Virginia, I asked some of the writers what was important to them in their writer's room. One told me she throws open the door of her studio every morning and sits on a chair in the doorway, feeling the light. A poet told me she never writes in one place. She finds the idea of regularity too confining. She writes in the car and in supermarkets, in cafés and trains, and always on scraps of paper. She told me large pieces of paper intimidate her. Another writer said she works in her husband's office on weekends. When I asked her why she didn't have a room of her own, she told me she had never wanted one. Her husband, a doctor, types all her manuscripts for her as she dictates from handwritten yellow legal pads. They enjoy the partnership.

This writer never intends to learn how to type. It might ruin her marriage. She has found her own balance. When I asked a journalist about her writer's room, she told me she has to have light and has to be able to see outside. She also requires two desks, one for her computer and one for editing, and a rolling chair in between to shift between the two. In addition, she needs a daybed with a good mattress. I know she lives in a large house, but I didn't ask her why she couldn't use her bedroom or the couches in the living room. It was clear she wanted this little nun-like bed in her writing room. That way, the door was closed and it was no one's business when she was having a little "lay-down."

One playwright told me "the quieter, the better" — dead silence. Another likes to look out on greenery and birds, "living things." Someone told of a playwright they knew who has to work with the curtains closed. He wants no part of the real world entering his writing world. Still another told me she never has pictures of family in her writing room. She finds them too intrusive. A lovely young Asian writer confessed she needs to feel "girly," and dresses that way when she writes. A playwright overhearing her conversation claimed to be the opposite. She wants to lose herself, to wear old clothes and kind of "schlump" around. The journalist, who grew up in Virginia and is an avid horsewoman, revealed she also finds it helpful to get dressed "professionally" when she's working. She dons a tweed jacket, ascot, riding britches, and boots, and off she goes into her writer's room. It puts her in the right mode. Still another writer, when asked about her room, told me that it was too private a question to answer. Her space was sacred, she told me, and that is as valid an answer as any.

It's clear that more than sharpening pencils, we need to prepare our workplaces to afford us optimum writing conditions. First, there are the tools that are necessities of our trade. Then there's the matter of technical expertise. We have to master the workings of our machinery, keep it in first-class condition, and be prepared for parts that periodically wear out. We should be knowledgeable about how to locate competent, affordable, and communicable technological help. Think of yourself as a small industry.

Many of us who bridged the transition from manual typewriters to computers swore we were happier with the former, that we enjoyed touching those wonderful old keys, down on "A," then let it spring back up, then "D," and so forth. Click, click, click. We went screaming into the computer age.

Now those of you who went like ducks to water into the modern world need not heed this. But for those who didn't, and who remain the hard core I finally mastered *Copy* and *Paste*, but please don't approach me yet with transferring to a PDF file, whatever that is. Read your manuals, keep the phone number of technical support help handy, and list the serial numbers of your computer(s), printers, scanners, and all relevant passwords. When you are on the road, bring all the above information with you. Next, do the tutorials. If you don't understand them, ask a friend or hire someone who does understand your computer program. You have to know how to change an ink cartridge (remember to take off the piece of tape from a new cartridge which prevents it from printing), as well as transfer a file through your e-mail. As writers we are expected to be technically literate. It is a mark of our professionalism and denotes self-respect.

Then, there's the question of the pen and pencil. I never met a playwright who wasn't in love with pens. Let me count the ways! My favorite pen is the green and gold Mont Blanc ballpoint, given to me by the dean of my school. The Uni-ball Vision Elite is a close second. I know some writers who are advocates of fountain pens and the entire filling ritual, together with specialized inks. Also, I don't know a playwright who is not in love with the ultra-fine Sharpie twin tip. And for some diehards, there is still the feather and ink method. But, do me a favor, and with apologies to the manufacturer, please, please, please dispose of all Bics and Bic-like pens collected from hotels and banks. As for pencils, there is only one writer's pencil: Truman Capote and many other writers favored the Berol's Black Warrior No. 2. It is a sturdy, soft, lead pencil. Take one in your hand and you'll never again go back to an ordinary yellow pencil. Give yourself permission to buy the pen of your dreams or, when someone asks you what you want for your birthday, be ready with the color, make, and model of your ideal writing tool. Be prepared. Start to read pen catalogues immediately.

It is this same kind of self-regard that fashions the rooms we work in. One workplace I had as a playwright was in an 1870 farmhouse we once owned in Connecticut. It was the old knotty pine birthing room. It was at the front of the house, was no larger than a closet, and had little light, due to an old pine tree that grew smack up against the window, compounded by dark walls. It was always winter in that room. Although I did love the coziness, and the feeling of being hugged by those walls, the darkness and isolation eventually did me in. The house had a formal dining room with a picture window overlooking the back meadow, so one day I moved my base of operations into the dining room, placing the dining table against the window. I was happier there because of the light, but the lack of privacy finally got to me. I was working in the middle of the house in a room without doors.

The house was on a quiet country road when we first bought it. It was next door to the home of Audrey Wood, the theatrical agent, who had Tennessee Williams among her clients. From our kitchen window you could see the spiral staircase that he had given Audrey from the set of *A Streetcar Named Desire*. It went up to a special writer's room she built for Mr. Williams. But soon after we moved in, Audrey Wood died, and new people came, and before I knew it, a tennis court was being built, obstructing the view of the spiral staircase. Soon after, the farmer across the meadow died, and his heirs sold the land to a contractor who divided it into six plots for mini-mansions. And that was the end of our quiet country road. After that, our town lost its originality, became more suburban, and slowly, the writers and artists moved away. I could never write there again. This place suddenly embodied everything I didn't want. When I moved to Manhattan the writing gates opened, and I was home.

For the past twenty years my writing has been done in our apartment in New York City's Greenwich Village. My writer's room, on the twenty-third floor, overlooks the Village, its shops, and students, bicycle riders, and taxis, all in constant motion. Beyond the Village is the glorious Hudson River. In winter, there are pieces of ice floating down in huge chunks, and in spring and summer, the boats — large passenger cruise ships on their way to foreign ports, the Circle Line with tourists aboard, sailboats and tugboats, and even the occasional kayak. But do I really see them? Once I am working, the world outside the window disappears. Yet, I believe I know it is all there. Much the same as a playwright has to know the world outside his stage set in order to bring it in at any moment, we also know what lies outside our rooms, and that becomes part of us and comforts us, if it is the right thing. I have a room with a view. I don't look out, but I feel the outside around me and am grateful for its light and activity. I am alone, but never lonely.

What else is in my room? Bookcases jammed with volumes, books by friends, favorite books, professional ones, ones I intend to read one day, or reread, plays and poems and novels and fairy tales and the three books passed down to me from my family as a child. There are shelves piled high with versions and revisions of manuscripts, rolling file drawers for current projects and research, and some for possible future projects. Then there are the journals, stacked in rows, those written in, and those, received as gifts or purchased as a "must have," waiting to be opened.

The walls are covered with corkboard in order to accommodate the dozens of photos from an ongoing writing life. Some are of grandchildren and some of friends; some are from productions and some from foreign travel or teaching. There are wall-to-wall photographs. They reassure me and strengthen me because they speak of how it all adds up.

My favorite photographs? One is of my husband, Don, the absolute love of my life, when he was a young sailor in Guantánamo Bay, Cuba. This was long before we knew what gifts life had in store for the two of us and that we would meet. Oh, yes, and on another wall is a photo of my father at seventeen as a sailor in Paris, and the one of my mother as a schoolgirl in Boston. Then there is the photo of my three daughters when they were young and I was twenty-three. There is the one of Barbara and I, two writer friends looking out to the Atlantic on the rocks outside her house in Gloucester, Massachusetts. Then there is the one of Tina and me in Maine, two writers lying on the grass, telling secrets. There is a favorite one of students from China waving sad goodbyes as we American teachers were leaving in 1987, after our appointed classes were finished. And the one of Aunt Rose who used to hold Sunday evening salons for writers and painters and composers at her beach house. At her table, on any given Sunday night, would be a dozen artists. I remember the cans of salmon she would open and the talk, the talk.

What are these photographs? They are our armor. They are the stuff that brought us on these journeys as writers. They are stories from our lives; same as our plays are stories. They are records of our beginnings and our perseverance. They give testimony that a writer lived here and it was us, and we acted on our dreams.

Memoirs and biographies abound with descriptions of artist's studios. One of my favorites is by Nancy Hale, great-granddaughter of the revolutionary patriot, Nathan Hale, and daughter of Edward Everett Hale, author of *The Man Without a Country*. An author in her own right, of books including *A New England Girlhood*, Hale writes in *A Life in the Studio*[2] about coming back to her mother's studio[2] after her mother's death. "Common sense and my advisors tell me I should get this old studio by the sea — which my aunt built, and where she and other artists painted and made etchings on a press set up under the skylight, where my mother painted for years after she inherited it, — with big north windows that I can use in everyday life."

Picture the ideal room where you would work. What does it have on the walls? What gives you, as a playwright, inspiration? Do you have quotes from other writers on the wall, printed on index cards? Do you like your room "lean and mean," rather Spartan, or filled with mementoes? Do you find music crucial or distracting while you are writing? I know a playwright who writes only to Mozart's *Requiem.* I know another who writes to recorded sounds of the sea.

If you can't have a complete room, can you make a space devoted just to you and your work as part of another room? It's not size or luxury which determines a writer's space, but more often elements of light, design, and especially, your personal imprint. Picture the ideal room for yourself as a playwright, and start to make it happen.

On top of my computer are all the amulets. There are the two storytellers from Santa Fe, the stones collected from the beaches of Martha's Vineyard to the Cape of Good Hope in South Africa. There are the crystals and the pieces of amber. There's the Indian penny and the fossil, the feather of a bluebird from Virginia and the small, flat silver heart with "passion" written across it, a gift for the opening of a production. There are, too, the medals my father won for battle in the First World War.

You are a warrior too. You are a writing warrior. And the things you place in your writer's room should bring you comfort and give you power. And if you're lucky, bring you luck.

This lecture was initially delivered at the University of London, June 1993, to a group of playwrights. It has been slightly revised for inclusion in this book.

Three Exercises in a Room of One's Own

1. The next time someone pays you for your playwriting, take part of the payment and purchase something from a visual artist. Hang it in your writer's room. Support the arts!

2. Devote three hours this week to reading all your manuals thoroughly. You may include your coffee pot and microwave. A writer has to drink and eat too.

3. Neaten and organize your office. Give it three hours. When you are finished, go to a stationary store and purchase something you always wanted — gold paper clips, Post-its to flag pages on scripts, yet another journal, or whatever your writer's heart desires.

3

FIFTY QUESTIONS TO ASK
WHEN WRITING A PLAY

When I start to write a play, I know the situation, the characters, and how I will begin the play. Sometimes, I know how I will end it. Sometimes I outline, sometimes not. The act of getting there is sometimes the surprise. If I knew everything about my play before I began, what would be the joy of writing it? We write to find out what it is we are writing about. We write by asking questions.

After a good amount of scenes are complete, I often think about the focus or the theme — what the play is about, which is different from the story. The story is the moving line. If, as I write, I find my characters straying too far from the focus, I either re-align my focus or my characters. As a playwright, I want to make certain we are all on the same boat.

In one popular formula for a play, you get your main character up a tree in the first act; in the second, you throw rocks at him; and in the third, you get him down from the tree. It is a case of structuring an escalating conflict that must be resolved: have someone want something, have someone else want something else, have them battle, and, win or lose, learn something in the process.

At the opening of every play, something must be happening and that something is the plot. Most plots are quite simple. It is the characters who make plays complex. Look at the plot, for example, of Tennessee Williams *The Glass Menagerie.* Amanda wants a suitor for her daughter, Laura. When Laura's brother Tom brings his friend Jim home for dinner, hopes are raised concerning Jim's potential as a "gentleman caller" for Laura, and then, hopes are dashed. It turns out that Jim is engaged.

I like to use simple plots that don't get in the way of the more important human interaction. If I make a plot outline before starting, I only utilize about one-third of what I plan. I like the security of the outline, but also want the license to travel wherever my characters might take me. After the first draft, and before beginning the rewrite, I always make an outline. But at this point I understand the play and its "weave" better.

But most of all, we construct plays by asking basic questions about character, plot, time span, location, speech pattern, stage design, style, and conflict. In our plays, we are also asking larger questions about what it means to be human. A play, after all, is the playwright questioning the universe.

The following is a series of questions I developed to be asked at the beginning of a project, throughout the first draft, at the end of the first draft, and again while rewriting. Most of the character-related questions are posited, for the playwright, at the start of the play. The thematic and story-oriented questions become most relevant partway through the play, just to make certain you *are* telling a story and that all the threads are pulling in the same direction.

No set of rules, especially in a creative medium, is expected to be followed with exactitude. We all know rules are made to be broken! There is no doubt you may write a strong and powerful play, breaking some of these rules. They are, however, helpful as guide-lines, a map for the unchartered territory of each play we write.

My fifty questions to develop a story are:

- Who are the characters in the play? Identify the major characters and the secondary characters.

- What is the history of each character, from birth? Compile a one-page biography for each character.

- What was each character doing in the twenty-four hours prior to the opening of the play? You need to know this in order to understand his or her emotional and physical condition when entering the play.

- What are the physical characteristics of each character? See each physically moving through the play. Cast your play with known actors or with real life people — friends, family, and colleagues.

- What does each character want in the play? Every character should want something very badly in a play and be prepared to fight for it. This is the character's objective.

- What is the objective of each character in every scene?

- Do the characters get what they want by the end of the play? If so, how does this affect them? If they do? If they don't? What resultant action comes from getting and not getting?

- What is each character's attitude toward the other people in the play? Who has the secret? What is it?

- Who is the hero or heroine? Is the hero or heroine the causer of action?

- What is the speech pattern of each character? Keep a journal jotting down snatches of conversation overheard. Listen to people's different cadences. Make certain each character has an absolutely individual voice.

- How does each character change during the action of the play? In a drama, characters must be in a different place at the end of the play than they were in the beginning. They should have been changed by the action of the play.

- What does each character learn from the change? Does he or she learn anything?

- What are each character's virtues and vices? Note that they are often one and the same. We rise and fall by the same qualities. For example, spontaneity is fine except when it turns to impulsiveness. A careful character may also fear taking risks and therefore miss opportunities. This is another way of finding the tragic flaw in the character.

- What do you like about each character? An author has to love the characters in some way to write about them. Even if the character is a villain there should be something likeable or you will lose your audience.

- What are the physical aspects of your set? You should see almost every object on the set, so when you write each scene you are able to use the objects on the set. If there is a live duck in the room, or a clock, or an apple, think how each could become significant in the action.

- What does the area outside the set consist of? Is it a street or the rest of a house? You need to know clearly the environs so that at any moment action can come in from outside onto your set.

- What will be the time span of your play? One month? One year? And why? What will this time span accomplish in terms of the action of the play?

- Where exactly does the action take place? What state or city or country? If it is specific it can add to your plot possibilities.

- What prompted you to begin this play? What do you think was the genesis? Was it an image? A line? An incident? Knowing where the play comes from helps keep focus.

- How can you translate the real incident that may have prompted your play into the best story? This entails changing some of the details and having narrative distance for the sake of the best drama. So, even if the heroine did get what she wanted in the real life story, on stage the play may work better if the heroine has larger obstacles but, try as she may, cannot overcome them.

- What is at stake in the play? This is what keeps the audience interested, so it must be something vital. That's why we call it drama.

- What are the escalating obstacles in the play?

- What are the dangers in the play? These must be set up at the very beginning. We should, as an audience, always

be in fear for the main character as we are for Oedipus.
We keep saying, "No Oedipus, don't do it!"

- What is the major action of the play? Tell the story of
  the play scene by scene.

- How does one scene push the next scene forward? The
  action in one scene should push the action in the next
  scene forward. There should be a domino effect, a cumu-
  lative sequence of events.

- What major question is this play positing? All strong
  plays ask important questions.

- Why do you think an audience will stay to hear your
  story? What is the suspense? Make certain the events
  and outcome are not predictable.

- What makes you anxious to tell this story? What is
  the pleasure for you? What questions are you trying to
  answer?

- Is there a message in the play and if so what is it as
  related to the characters and their actions? Is it that
  greed leads to destruction? Is it that anger can grow into
  revenge and then into fury and then into murder, so
  beware? Understand what your moral stance is and the
  statement you are trying to make.

- What moment draws the audience in at the beginning of
  the play, the first five pages? Why?

- What is the style of the play? Is it realistic or absurd? Is
  that style evident in the very beginning of the play and is
  it consistent?

- What is motivating the characters in the play and how far will they go to get what they want? Will they kill or steal for it? Die or betray for it?

- Are you creating an identifiable but also unique world?

- Are the major actions happening on stage and not off stage? Don't put the major actions of the play in a speech. Show, don't tell.

- Does every confrontation lead to resolution?

- Does the action (the plot) of the play represent the thematic statement you would like to posit with this play?

- What will the audience be able to relate to in the play? Will they identify with each character's experiences and resultant actions?

- Is the major action of the play clear? If it is, the play will have focus. The audience and the playwright then can clearly state what the play is about.

- Is the subject of the play substantial so that it earns its time in the theater? Remember the enormous physical, emotional, and financial outlay that goes into every production.

- Is there humor in the play? Humor is release from the intensity of the action, even in the most serious of tragedies. The best humor comes not from a funny line but from the intrinsically comedic action of the character.

- What are the critical turning points in the play?

- Where is the climax of the play? If there were a graph plotting the rising action, where is the highest moment? After this moment, everything changes and there is no turning back.

- Are you certain you have begun the play at the right time? Would the story be better served if you began it earlier or later? What then is the best moment to begin this play so that the most dramatic action is shown on stage? For example, if the boy is going to cut down the only cherry tree in front of the house, you would not start the play *after* he cuts it down but rather in the time period leading up to his cutting the tree down and then show the resultant action.

- Do all the characters have a reason to stay in the play? What is keeping them there?

- Is this play unique in the way it tells the story?

- If it is a one-act play, what is the one major event of the play?

- If it is a two-act play, does the first act end with a large question that is answered in the second act? Likewise between acts two and three.

- If the characters chose a different action in their confrontation of the obstacles, how might that change in the resultant action? What would that different choice mean thematically? Choose the action that defines the theme. It is individual choice that informs all tragedy.

- Do you love this play enough to commit to a very long period of planning, writing, rewriting, and hopefully production with all its attendant angst and satisfaction? The road will be predictably treacherous. Do you want to make the journey with this play?

This lecture was delivered to a group of professional writers at the Beijing Film School, Beijing, China, June 1987. Excerpts are from "Writing a Stage Play," published in The Writer's Handbook, The Writer, Inc., Boston, Mass., Sylvia Burack, Editor, 1990, 1995. Is has been slightly revised for inclusion in this book.

Exercise on the Fifty Questions

Answer all fifty questions, as well as you can, at the start of your play. Answer all fifty questions again, in the middle of your play. Then answer these same questions at the completion of the first draft, and the next time you pick it up to begin rewriting. It's a continual process of demanding answers to the play's questions.

4
CHARACTER

What is character? Where is it born? What gives us courage? What makes us prideful? What do we yearn for? What would we kill for? What makes one person stand erect and the other stooped? Why will one run from danger and the other run into it? What gives each of us our uniqueness, our own sound, our character? These are the questions every playwright must answer before beginning his or her script because dramatic pieces, above all, are about people — what they do and why they do it. Plays are about events happening between people and as such are grounded in the reality of the characters who are participating in those special events.

For an hour or two during a play, an intimate relationship is established between the audience and the characters on stage. However, with certainty, the audience cannot be deceived. The people in the story may be acting, but they must be acting out the particularities of the lives of real people. Therefore, a dramatic writer must know his or her characters in the most intimate of ways. He or she must know what each person would do in any given situation and how that person came to act in such a manner; how the person became the person he or she is. Most important, the writer must love that person for whom he or she is with all his or her particularities and flaws.

Character is defined not by what you say, but by what you do. During the writing of the play, you choose those actions in every scene to substantiate your characterization. A character is *always* defined by his or her *actions*. Character *is* action. During the process of creation, you must come to know your characters so well that they will virtually write your script for you. It will always be the character speaking, then, and not the author. I experienced this when writing my first play, *Statues*, a one-act play about the meeting between a sculptor of religious statuary, Roberto Da Fralizzi, and a high school teacher, Jennie Ames, who comes to his statue factory to borrow a piece of statuary for the school play she is directing. I knew only vaguely that these two would get together by the end of the play, but the "how," the particulars, I did not know. When Da Fralizzi, three quarters through the play asks, "Jennie, you like calamari?" I could hardly believe it. He was asking her to dinner. I hadn't anticipated he would do that. He had taken on his own life. His words were rushing out at such a speed I could hardly keep up with them on the typewriter. George Bernard Shaw describes the same phenomenon when writing *St. Joan*.

After the generating moment of the dramatic story, which is essentially the situation, I then choose the people who will inhabit the world I am creating, and for each character, I draw up an elaborate biography.

Who is she? What does she look like? Where does she come from? Was she pretty when she was little? Did she have friends? What was her favorite toy? Did she have a tree she liked to sit under? What books did she read? What are her summer memories? How did she feel the day she was married, when her first child was born, when her mother died?

In her life now, preceding the moment when she stepped onto the stage and into the story, where was she? What does she have for breakfast and does she hear the birds singing in the morning? Is she a good tennis player and does she polish her fingernails and what is her favorite flower? What does she wish was different in her life? Does she like to hike and can she sew a button on so that it's secure? Could she take a vacation alone? Is she frigid or frivolous or neither? Would she lie? Does she like animals? Has she come to terms with the idea of her own mortality? I want to know the color of her hair and eyes and the shape of her limbs and if she has a birthmark.

How does she carry herself? What is her walk? Initially, I have to see her; then I want to understand her. I want to know about her lifestyle. What kind of neighborhood was she brought up in? Did she live on a wide tree-lined street, bordered with white houses and well-clipped hedges or was it a working-class neighborhood? And how did she feel about the place where she grew up, the society in which she moved? If it was lower class, did she know it? Did she aspire to more? Did she eventually move up? Why and how? I always look for the roots, because people carry the past on their backs.

What does she do to earn her way in the world? Is her work filled with possibilities or boredom? Where did she go to school? What were her grades? What was written about her in the school yearbook? The questions tumble on. Specificity gives the character a reality.

Ask yourself some basic questions about your character. Where does she stand politically and religiously? What is her basic philosophy and morality? I also like to know what magazines and books my character reads — not what she tells her friends she reads, but what she takes away on vacation. It says almost everything about us.

"What are your favorite books?" I ask the character. Tell me in order of one to ten. *Pride and Prejudice* or any Jane Austen one would say, *Gone With the Wind* another, *The Wind in the Willows* another ... and you know a little piece of who they are. There is no room for inaccuracy in this biography. You are the creator and therefore, the knower. Maybe you can identify more about the character than the character can about him- or herself. After all, it's the writer, the creator, who understands the strengths and weaknesses that cause the character to act in the fashion that reveals these basic traits.

The fictive power is awesome and the writer has the responsibility of making order of a life and all its uniqueness. What are the character's ambitions? Get inside his dreams. What's gone wrong? Have your character talk to you and tell you about the greatest disappointment of his life. Nothing will so get to the heart of the vulnerabilities of your character and his humanity than an honest answer to his question. I also ask my character what was the happiest day of his life. It tells me something about what works for him — power, love, peaceful isolation.

Each of us has our own watering hole, the place that feeds us, and each character, through his or her actions, accumulates a unique biography. Arthur Miller points out in his play, *The Price*, that we invent ourselves. In creating a character, you fill a space in the universe that formerly went unused. To create means to make what was not there before.

What is the attitude of the character toward the actions of her life? How does she view herself? How does she view life? Does she really love her husband? Her children? Is she superstitious? Is her house tidy? Did her mother love her? Does she know her mother loved her? What does she wish for in the deep of the night? What will or could happen to her?

Every time I go past the bridge over the Merrimack River, which looks westward toward the small town of Pepperell, Massachusetts, where Jennie Ames, the schoolteacher in *Statues* was born, I give a small wave to her. I believe she somehow lives out there, although I fabricated her entire life story.

What characterizes a person, tells us what makes him or her an individual? We are, as examined by J. Bronowski in *The Identity of Man*[1], a machine by birth, but an individual through experience.

Sitting on a train or a bus, for example, look around you. The boy next to you is wearing blue jeans, but with a neat green cotton shirt embroidered with an alligator. He eats a carton of yogurt and reads a paperback copy of *Gulliver's Travels*. He tells you he is reading the book for school. "I like yogurt," he tells you also, and then later, "My father says *Gulliver's Travels* is really a very political book, but I shouldn't worry about that now, so I'm not."

You learn later during the ride that his grandmother has a summer house on Deer Island in Maine and that the young man is going to visit the daughter of his father's college roommate (Princeton, class of 1976) and will be taking her to her "Senior Cotillion." Chances are this boy is conservative, rich, well educated, still listens to his father, likes girls, and likes healthy food. That's all the information we have about him. This is what he selects to give us. The writer, then, given the known, must fill in the unknown. He must make a full shape, given the base, being realistic and unique at the same time. Unpredictable, but still reasonable.

What about the girl, then, across the aisle? She is wearing a thin white cotton blouse, a bright red cotton skirt, and sandals, her long straight blond hair falling midway down her back, her blue eyes wide as she animatedly talks to the young disc jockey (or so he said he was) who sits down beside her. "I want to be a stewardess," she says. She is seventeen. "I think if I had to die, I'd want to die in a car accident — real fast — but in a Porsche." She goes on to say that she just gave up cigarette smoking that morning and that she loves to dance and that she hates boring people. "Like adults. Boring people really bore me," she says.

You are writing all this down in the journal you carry, the exact dialogue, because it is like gold, and because you will not remember it verbatim. You are getting down the words in their exact order because not only do they characterize the young girl, but they also tell us her special speech pattern, her rhythm. Rhythm is the particular manner in which a character strings his or her words together.

The young disc jockey, who claims he's on a diet (she can't understand why), asks her for her phone number. She describes the road to her home on Long Island, New York, lined with copper beeches, and at the end of the drive, a large white stucco house, with elegant gardens to the right. It sounds straight out of *The Great Gatsby*.

The disc jockey then goes to buy her a Coke and the young conductor on the train sits down, telling her he went to Amherst College, which is in western Massachusetts, but he left in his junior year and maybe he'll go back. You're writing all of this down in your journal. He claims he is really a writer, however, "mostly essays ... mostly everything." She looks bored.

You wonder about how much he really writes. You wonder about the young girl. The predictables are easy — the moneyed life, the easy life. You look at her. Now she's asleep. The disc jockey has gotten off long ago. She breathes easily. What's her secret? You wonder if maybe she doesn't really want to be a stewardess. Maybe she wishes she could go to college if she hadn't flunked senior English. She told the disc jockey she kind of "cruised around" senior year, so those bridges are burnt behind her ... or are they?

In her voice, you detect a wistfulness, a yearning that even she hasn't seen yet. This is what you're following. You are a detective, always looking for the small shiver, the portion of the iceberg not showing. It's the writer's job to fill in the gaps. A writer asks two questions when developing a character: What? and What if?

When you are certain you know your characters completely and passionately, that you have come to love, respect, and understand them, much like some kind of a marriage contract, then you are ready to begin writing.

Once you know your characters' voices, you must plan why they speak in every scene. The playwright must, as every character speaks, become that character. Schizophrenic? Yes. I explain the process as jumping into the computer with the character. For example, when I am writing Alma's speech, I physically become her, sitting in my chair exactly as she would, and likewise for Zaza or for Sam. I may change my position six times in one page, depending on the number of characters speaking. You must lose the writer and gain as many personalities and particularities of their emotions as appear in your play.

The writer must choose situations which best reveal a character's strengths and weaknesses. You must test them. For example, imagine that a woman had decided, after a long and miserable marriage, to leave her husband. He then develops cancer. What will she do? Not, what would anyone do, but what would this particular woman do? Everyone has a biography and because of that unique accumulation, we act specifically in a situation.

Now this particular woman is honest and loyal and has a strong sense of integrity, so the internal conflict is considerable. But you, the writer, know all the major moments of her life preceding this decision. You know that she was brought up in a strict and unloving home, that she has a strong religious background, that her high school years were quiet and uneventful, that her college years were marked by a loving relationship with a man outside her religion, that her parents disapproved, that she married another man, that her marriage turned out to be disappointing and loveless, and that the one son resulting from this marriage had turned out poorly and was in jail in Florida. You also know that she was loyal to this husband long after there was nothing to be loyal and loving about — a bleak landscape, marked with a taste of possibility, inhabited by a woman of strength and courage, but not stupidity. She will leave her sick husband and it may be the bravest thing she's ever done. You know that she is ready to choose in favor of herself. You also know the decision will not come easily, but given what has come before, you understand the reasons for her actions and will bring the audience, hopefully, to the same understanding.

What you do, essentially, once your characterization is complete, is devise plot situations that will test your character. This is why you must know just how far each person will go to get what he or she wants. The possibilities of human behavior are infinite. It is a question of selection that heightens the dramatic conflict.

Characters in a drama should be in opposition to the situation. Don't make it easy for anyone. That's boring. And choose the unexpected: the little man, not the general, leading the troops into battle; the conservative opting for the largest risk; the doctor who is not so humanitarian.

Choose a new configuration. Go to a greenhouse; look at the variety of plants. Think about the factors influencing their future. How will they be tested? What will define them? How will they grow? Characters are defined by what they *do*.

It is the work of the playwright to create a character of unequivocal interest and uniqueness, to create that character with affection, and to know how and why that character will act in any given circumstance. Then, the dramatist should construct the situation and action of the play with adequate conflict, with the major characters being in opposition to one another, so as to dramatically depict the very center or soul of each person. George Balanchine used to say that only God creates; the artist reveals.

For many playwrights, character is the single most important element in a play. Arthur Miller maintained that all of his plays began with a fascination with a particular character and his story.

After the initial creation of the character, you are in the second step of the process. Now the drama has to test the character's strengths and weaknesses. On a hot day, after all, you put the cold punch in the front room where everyone can taste it, not in the back pantry. So, if the major character in your play is driven by greed, there must be a pile of gold to be had and fought over. If another character is defined by her dignity, let her fall as hard as she can and see how she holds her head up. Let each character's strengths be tested; let dignity flourish in adversity and persistence in failure. Give the character a war to be fought and a reason to show his or her mettle. Give another character something she wants, then give her something standing in the way of that desire, and then watch her fight. You alone know what weapons they will use in battle, because you, the author, are the only one who knows your characters with certainty. After all, you created them.

When we initially conceive a character, we, as playwrights, are following them. Eventually, after spending time with your characters, hopefully, they will lead you. The idea is, through the writing process, to become closer and closer to your characters, and that way, closer to the heart of the play.

This lecture was delivered to a group of writers at Harvard University, Cambridge, Massachusetts, in January 1978. It has been slightly revised for inclusion in this book.

Three Exercises in Character Development

1. First, give your character a name. Then, cast your character, either with someone you know or with a well-known actor in theatre or film. This will give your character a physicality and help you visualize the character "moving" through the play. As you go along, change the name if it doesn't suit the character.

2. Next, keep a journal, devoting one full week to your character. The character should be with you wherever you are. Record what the character does as he/she encounters each situation. What does she eat for breakfast? What magazines does he read? Does she have a dog she has to walk? Does he have a lover who calls? What are their plans for tonight? For the weekend? What does she do for exercise? What is his profession and is he successful and does he like it? What is an average day like for each character?

3. Then, ask your character to answer the following questions:
   What was the happiest day in your life so far?
   What was the saddest day?
   What was the most difficult day?
   What are you most proudest of?

Answer these questions in your character's voice. The answers will cut to the center of the character's soul and vulnerabilities, telling you what that person would fight for, what would give him conflict, what would give her joy. The character will be revealing to you, the writer, his or her deepest secrets. Plays, after all, are about our characters' secrets — secrets they keep from one another and secrets they keep from themselves.

5

DIALOGUE: THE WAYS OUR CHARACTERS SPEAK TO US

Dialogue is the playwright's fundamental tool. It's the major way we connect with our audiences. Many playwrights tell me that the reason they chose to write for the theater was their passion and talent for dialogue. If pressed, I could write descriptions of a trip I took recently through the Blue Ridge Mountains, talking about the redbuds in bloom and the shadows on the mountains, but that's not what interests the playwright most. Living people do — what they *say* and *why they say it*.

In plays, characters have two kinds of dialogue always at work. The actual words that come out of their mouths, what they *choose* to say, comprise the exterior dialogue. The interior dialogue is what the character is actually thinking and feeling — the subtext. These two kinds of dialogue are as different as oranges and apples, and the intrinsic meaning between what a character is saying and what a character is thinking and feeling is at the center of all plays. That place where the interior dialogue intersects with the exterior is the moment of explosion in all plays. It is the instant when the character can no longer contain his or her real feelings.

Playwright Tony Kushner says that the difference between a good playwright and a bad playwright is caring about every single word that comes out of a character's mouth. David Mamet, that master of dialogue, in a speech before the Dramatists Guild Projects Committee and the Stage Directors and Choreographers Foundation, said that characters on stage do not speak to reveal themselves, but rather to conceal themselves. Mamet claims they speak to get whatever it is they want. It is an excellent exercise to go through one of your plays and see how many times this holds true. It will also serve as a checkpoint, ensuring that your characters have something they want in every scene. It is a primary tenet of playwriting: without desire there is no action.

George Pierce Baker, a professor of English at Harvard University from 1888 to 1924, instituted the now legendary 47 Workshop in Drama in 1904. Baker taught, among dozens of students, Eugene O'Neill, Sidney Howard, Thomas Wolf, and Philip Barry. Entrance standards were extraordinarily high, and admission was granted only to those showing true promise as dramatists. In his book *Dramatic Technique*, published in 1919, Baker says:

> Modern dramatic dialogue had beginnings far from reality. It originated, as the Latin tropes show, in speeches given in unison and to music — a kind of recitative. What was the aim of this earliest dramatic dialogue? It sought to convey ... the facts of the episode or incident represented. And that is what good dramatic dialogue has always done, is doing, and must always do as its chief work — state clearly the facts which an audience must understand if the play is to move ahead steadily and clearly. ... When a dramatist works as he should, the emotion of his characters give him the right words for carrying their feelings to the audience, and every word counts. ... The more real

the emotion the more compact and connotative ... is its expression.[1]

A good exercise in dialogue writing is to go through an ordinary day in your own life, marking in your journal, hour by hour, what you are doing and what you want. Our "wants" are complex in one twenty-four-hour period. We wake up and we want music, or solitude, or coffee, or the news, or we are lonely and want companionship, or we want to get some work done, or we want a long bath, or we want to go back to bed. A few hours later we are at work and we want an excuse to leave, or we want to procrastinate, so we find ourselves cleaning a closet, or we have a deadline and are working under pressure, and at the same time we have planned a clandestine affair at lunch, and we want to get there, because it makes us feel wanted, or sexy, or dangerous — whatever it is we want to feel. Now we have a conflict. We want to successfully complete our work project and gain praise from our boss, or we want to succeed for our own sense of self-esteem, or we think success may auger a raise in pay; but we also want love in our lives, or lived fantasy, or whatever it is we desire of this particular relationship. But what will our dialogue consist of in specific situations? What will be the choices for your characters in any given scene in your play? It depends on your character and what he or she wants most. The action will grow out of the desire, and Mamet is right — what the character then says is directly related to what he is trying to get.

In my play *After Marseilles*, set in a postapocalyptic world, Sam wants to elicit information from Madame Zaza. What he wants is for her to admit she has been lying to him. What she wants is to evade Sam's questions.

Sam: I went over the bridge while you were gone. I met someone who knows you.

Zaza: Everyone knows me. I'm well known.

Sam:	A Mr. Sanderson.
Zaza:	An Algerian malcontent if I ever saw one.
Sam:	He said it's rumored the government in Paris is in disarray.
Zaza:	Nonsense. There's a woman in Paris with red hair who tells us what to do.
Sam:	What's her name?
Zaza:	We don't know. Miss. I call her "Miss."
Sam:	And who put this woman with red hair in charge?
Zaza:	She said she was. Don't question me.
Sam:	But who appointed her? Someone must have appointed her.
Zaza:	I'm telling you, the government. I tried to charm the shrew, but she was like a steam roller.
Sam:	But you could charm a warthog, Zaza.
Zaza:	Not this one. She's ill tempered and officious.
Sam:	But who appointed her?
Zaza:	She said the government.
Sam:	WHAT GOVERNMENT?
Zaza:	I DON'T KNOW!

This is an example of the interplay between dialogue and wants. The two characters are sparring with each other, and what a dance it is. Sam finally breaks Zaza down and the entire play explodes at that point, with Zaza being exposed as a liar.

If dialogues often comes out of motivation to conceal or reveal or acquire, and at the same time reveals character and moves the plot, then the larger task for the dramatist is to make that dialogue real, and yet, at the same time, true to the voice of each character. Every line must be written as only that character would speak it. How do you achieve this kind of reality?

Not every playwright is born with what I call a "Mametian" ear. Some of us have ears like tape recorders, and others have to practice. In order to perfect a character's voice I suggest keeping a journal of overheard conversations and marking them down verbatim. They are a storehouse of gold. They are records of individual dialects and rhythms and word choices. I think of it as each character having his or her own poetry. In addition, I am always looking for the phrase or sentence that gives away a person's truth. You tell a friend you need someone to talk to and they tell you they are busy on a project deadline, but "Next Tuesday afternoon they are free." Doesn't that say it all. We give ourselves away continually.

In Tina Howe's memorable *Painting Churches*, Fanny, originally played by Marian Seldes, remembers love and breathes desire in the following speech to her daughter, Mags:

> There were real snow storms in the old days. Not these pathetic little two-inch droppings we have now. After a particularly heavy one, Daddy and I used to go sledding on the Common. This was way before you were born. … God, it was a hundred years ago! … Daddy would stop writing early, put on these galoshes and come looking for me, jingling the fasteners like castanets. It was a kind of a mating call, almost. The Common was always deserted after a storm; we had the whole place to ourselves. It was so romantic. Daddy would lie down on the sled, I'd lower myself on top of him, we'd rock back and forth a few times to gain momentum and then … WHOOOOOOOOSSSSSHHHH … down we'd plunge like a pair of eagles locked in a spasm of love-making.[3]

Lanford Wilson, one of the most authentic dialogue writers in the American theater, catches his characters' speech flawlessly in *The Hot l Baltimore*, and, in such variety, it makes your head spin. The following speech belongs to one of the residents of the Hotel Baltimore, the "e" long burnt out of the marquee, also giving us a clue to the play's major theme of loss. In this vintage Wilson speech that captures his sense of both comedy and wistfulness, the character of Suzy speaks:

> I love champagne because you got to share it with people; sittin' around drinking champagne all by yourself without an event would be like jerkin' off.[4]

In an early play of mine, *Exhibition*, the character of Katy Valentine, a former Rockette at Radio City Music Hall, or so she says, describes herself like this: "I get up every morning and I shake that tree and I say, 'Come on, day, come on day, give me a surprise.' And if no surprise happens, I make it happen (*snapping her fingers*) just like that. Life's a chef's salad, man. You gotta dig right in. Otherwise, it's a drag."[5]

How do you get these voices so exact and unique so that they could only possibly belong to the given character and are distinct from everyone else's voice in the play? I said you had to hear the character speak to you, you might ask how one gets the character to speak. The best exercise I know is asking the character a leading question, any question, and asking the character to answer in his or her own voice. The schizophrenic ear and pen of the writer are tuned into the particularity of each character's voice. Until you hear that voice, you can't write that play. It will only be the playwright speaking and never your characters.

In writing a play, you are following three lines: the brain, the mouth, and the heart. When devising dialogue, I am trying to follow these three lines through each speech. Often, these lines are running a far distance from one another. It's only when they finally intersect, when what the character is thinking and feeling coalesce and explode into the spoken word that we get the rise of the dramatic action.

What fascinates me about playwriting is how what people are saying often has nothing to do with what they actually mean. This means that you are continually asked to interpret the subtext. It is almost like translating a foreign language. The words are the text and the subtext is what we know they are thinking. In this way, they are indeed, as Mamet says, concealing. Listen for the ways people choose to hide information, and like a translator, learn to convert subtext to text, so meaning is discernable but not visible. In drama we keep away from the obvious. It is as if we were trying to think up one hundred ways to say "No," without saying that exact word, at the same time meaning that we are open to negotiation.

Often I begin from what the character is thinking and then try to translate it into a line of text that belies the real meaning, but that our audience can interpret. For example, a character in a play can be thinking about another character, "I hate you." But he doesn't say this. He says something else, which can mean, "I don't like or respect you, and if I had a chance, I would sabotage and betray you." For this reason, real life is an excellent laboratory for the playwright.

Often character becomes profoundly clear. Someone speaks simply one line and you know almost everything about that person, because you are an interpreter, always listening for the real meaning. It is one of the most challenging language exercises I know. Every morning I go out into the world and there it is, people inadvertently revealing themselves.

For example, you are sharing a hotel room with a friend whom you do not know well, and you are shivering. The friend asks if you are okay. You tell the person the temperature is too cool, and you hold out one of your almost frozen fingers for him or her to touch. Instead of offering to raise the temperature, the person tells you he or she is much too hot. Then you are admonished for not wearing the right clothes. You eventually leave because you are so cold. Each line has an exterior and an interior dialogue. The scene would go something like this:

Margaret: It's freezing in here. (I'm cold.)
Ann: Is it now? (I don't care.)

Margaret: Just feel my hands. They're like icicles. (Don't you
             believe me?)

Ann: Well I'm hot. Boy, when I'm hot, I get such head-
             aches. (I'm not changing the temperature, even if
             you ask.)

Margaret: Could you put up the heat just a little? (You witch,
             I'm putting it to you.) I'm so cold I'm going to get
             sick. (I'm playing the pity and compassion card.)

Ann: You brought the wrong clothes. (You idiot you,
             you dolt. If you had brought the right clothes you
             wouldn't be so cold.)

Margaret: What's the temperature at now? (I am *not* going out
             to buy new clothes. It's you who is going to have to
             make the adaptation.)

Ann: I don't know. (I am not moving to read the thermo-
             stat.)

Margaret: (*Going over to the thermostat*) It's at sixty-two. (I can't
             believe how mean you are being.)

Ann: You need to go down the road and buy yourself a
             sweater. (I am not budging. I told you what to do.
             Now go and do it.)

Margaret: Don't tell me what I need! I need to get out of here
             is what I need!

Note that on the last line, Margaret can no longer keep a lid on what she's feeling, and the actual dialogue catches up with her legitimate rising anger. What's interesting in this simple scene is how long both hold off from saying what they actually mean.

Anton Chekhov is considered by many to be the quintessential user of subtext as a dramatic tool. Unlike in the scene above, the character's true feelings never emerge in words. In his last play, *The Cherry Orchard*, the Ranevsky family is preparing to move out of their house because they can no longer afford to keep it. The businessman, Lopakhin, has bought their estate, and workers are chopping down their cherry orchard as the play comes to an end. He and the Ranevsky's adopted daughter, Varya, have been avoiding the subject of marrying each other — and since Lopakhin has bought the estate, and Varya is forced to take a housekeeping position far from her family, the logical course of events is that he propose to her. Varya's mother pushes her into a room alone with Lopakhin; this is what happens:

> *(A few stifled laughs and whispers behind the door.*
> *Finally Varya enters.)*
> *There is a restrained laugh behind the door, a whisper,*
> *then Vayra comes in.*

Varya: (*Looking at the luggage in silence*) I can't seem to find it. . . .

Lopakhin: What are you looking for?

Varya: I packed it myself and I don't remember. (Pause.)

Lopakhin: Where are you going to now, Barbara Mihailovna?

Varya: I? To the Ragulins. . . . I've got an agreement to go and look after their house . . . as housekeeper or something.

Lopakhin: Is that at Yashnevo? It's about fifty miles. (Pause) So life in this house is finished now. . . .

Varya: (*Looking at the luggage*) Where is it? . . . perhaps I've put it away in the trunk. . . Yes, there'll be no more life in this house. . . .

Lopakhin: And I'm off to Kharkov at once . . . by this train. I've a lot of business on hand. I'm leaving Ypikhodov here . . . I've taken him on.

Varya: Well, well!

Lopakhin: Last year at this time the snow was already falling, if you remember, and now it's nice and sunny. Only it's rather cold. . . . There's three degrees of frost

Varya: I didn't look. (*Pause*) And our thermometer's broken. . . . (*Pause.*)

Voice at the door: Ermolai Alexeyevitch!
Lopakhin: (As if he has long been waiting to be called) This
                minute.
                (*Exit quickly.*)
                Varya, sitting on the floor, puts her face on a bundle of
                clothes and weeps gently

So much for that marriage.

The trick with dialogue is the sparity, except for the occasional monologue. You are not a tape recorder, and just because a line is real is no reason to put it in a play. Reality is never an excuse for art. If we want reality, we can open our windows and listen.

Good dialogue is about selectivity, and the challenge is in finding those words which intimate advancing thunder and trouble. Every line a character utters should either enhance characterization or move the plot. Otherwise, if you have a good line, put it on a post card.

This lecture was delivered at New York University's International Program, Writing Prague, June 2001. It has been slightly modified for inclusion in this book.

Exercises in Dialogue Writing:

Take the following three speeches and rewrite them making them as boring as possible, with flat language, overwriting, banality, triteness, clichés, etc. When you are finished, take a good look at this bad writing and promise never to write like this again.

1. Ella from Sam Shepard's *Curse of the Starving Class:*
   Do you know what this is? It's a curse. I can feel it. It's invisible but it's there. It's always there. It comes onto us like nighttime. Every day I can feel it. Every day I can see it coming. And it always comes. Repeats itself. It comes

even when you do everything to stop it from coming.
Even when you try to change it. And it goes back. Deep. It
goes back and back to tiny little cells and genes. To atoms.
To tiny little swimming things making up their minds
without us. Plotting in the womb. Before that even. In the
air. We're surrounded with it. It's bigger than the government even. It goes forward too. We spread it. We pass it
on. We inherit it and pass it down, and then pass it down
again. It goes on and on like that without us.[7]

2. Song from David Henry Hwang's *M. Butterfly*:
It's one of your favorite fantasies, isn't it? The submissive
oriental woman and the cruel white man ... consider it
this way; what would you say if a blonde homecoming
queen fell in love with a short Japanese businessman? He
treats her cruelly, then goes home for three years, during
which time she prays to his picture and turns down marriage from a young Kennedy. Then, when she learns he
has remarried, she kills herself. Now, I believe you would
consider this girl to be a deranged idiot, correct? But
because it's an oriental who kills herself for a westerner
— ah — you find it beautiful.[8]

3. Pale from Lanford Wilson's *Burn This*:
Goddamn this fuckin' place, how can anybody live in
this shit city? I'm not doin' it. I'm not drivin' my car in
this goddamn sewer every fuckin' time. Who are these
assholes? The city's got this space specially reserved for
his private use. Twenty-five fuckin' minutes I'm driving
around this garbage street; I pull up to this space, I look
back, this fuckin' baby-shit green Trans-Am's on my ass
going BEEP BEEP. I get out, this fucker says, "That's my
space." I showed him the fuckin' tire iron, I told the fucker.
You want this space, you're gonna wake up tomorrow, find

you slept in your fuckin' car. This ain't your space. Am I right? There's no talkin' to shit like that.[9]

Now, take the following three ordinary lines and rewrite them. Make the language original, spirited, specific, and anything but boring.

1. I get so angry when you act like that, like you don't even care about me.
2. I think I'm falling in love with you.
3. We must stop seeing each other like this, in secret.

6

LOCATION: PASSPORTS TO PLAYWRIGHTING

In Eugene O'Neill's *Long Day's Journey into Night*, the foghorn blows and we can smell the salt air off the coast of New London, Connecticut; at the same time, the fog shrouds the characters in their ghostlike lives. In all of Tennessee Williams's plays, the Southern heat clings to the sheets and wearies the characters trying to fight their way to love. The Bakersfield, California, of Sam Shephard's plays is as arid in landscape as the characters that populate them. Like the local earth itself, the characters' efforts to make a living have left them depleted and angry, tearing at one another. In John Guare's *Six Degrees of Separation*, the New York life of glamour, celebrity and reinvention, is only possible in this city that has spawned such a culture. Location is all.

For centuries, the idea has existed that our state of well-being and our conflicts are shaped as much by place as they are by neuro-chemistry and heredity. Hippocrates, two thousand years ago, as a major tenet of Western medicine, established that our bodies and minds are affected by location.[1] As playwrights we are aware of those locations that will be dangerous for our characters. In drama we're not concerned with joy and comfort, because plays are not about happy people. Plays are more likely about the impossible striving for joy or the unjust loss of bliss, or the tragedy that results from individual choice. It is always about the battle.

The power of location in our plays requires that we put our characters in environments that test them. It can be a place that triggers unconscious childhood memories, or can involve climate, politics, economics, or transition. For example, when I think of the gentrification occurring in this country, I think about the long-time residents who thought their children would be able to buy houses up the street, and back doors could be left unlocked. They are being tested. Place your play in an explosive location for your characters.

Arthur Miller's *The Price* takes place in the attic of a Manhattan brownstone, soon to be torn down. The place is cluttered with furniture, relics of a lifetime of living. Two brothers come together with the ancient Solomon, a furniture appraiser, to see what price they could get for the "stuff." The location is both claustrophobic and crushing, and going through the objects — an old sculling oar, a bed, a pair of ice skates — forces the brothers, as Miller says, to demand "of one another what was forfeited to time."[2] By locating the play as he does, Miller forces memory. It's ingenious — no sets, no dreams — just "stuff."

In Eugene O'Neill's *The Iceman Cometh*, the action takes place at a bar in New London, Connecticut, home territory for the playwright. According to Arthur and Barbara Gelb's biography of O'Neill, the location was probably inspired by a saloon on Fulton Street, New London, called Jimmy the Priest's and the ramshackle hotel in Greenwich Village, The Golden Swan.[3] For O'Neill, the bar setting allowed a disparate group of characters to converge, and to come and go, while alcohol induced truth and illusion.

To locate a play is to find the nucleus of the play, to give the characters a specific grounding both on the set and in the areas surrounding the set. After the playwright decides on the characters that will inhabit the play, the next decision is location. The "where" helps determine both the expectations and the possible and probable conflicts.

Playwrights such as Beckett and Ionesco have successfully placed their plays nonspecifically with careful detail to atmosphere only. For example, in Ionesco's *The Chairs* he describes simply "somber decor, in gray monotones. A messy room."[4] If your play is deliverately written without specificity of location, the details, of necessity, must be posited in the landscape and be integral to the axis of the play.

As part of locating the play, think about what atmosphere will raise the stakes for your characters, escalating the conflicts. Plays are never about comfortable people. What would give your protagonist the most problems? Maybe they are far from home. When you are away from home, what issues does that raise for you? What can be the dangers? Or maybe they are at a sister's house and they don't like that sister. What if they were just moving into a new space? How about a bad hotel room? I once placed two people on their honeymoon in a run down hotel on the French Riviera. By the end of the short play *Sunday at Five on the Cote D'Azur*, you know the marriage will never last. I knew that my main character, who was given to "blue" moods on Sunday afternoons, would never make it through the disappointment of this tacky hotel room. Of course it was more than the hotel room.

An example of the use of specific location is found in my first produced play, *Statues*. The hunter in me had always wanted a reason to enter the wide-windowed world of a religious statue factory in Charlestown, Massachusetts, that I passed on my daily ride on Boston's elevated train. I had an idea for a play. Shortly thereafter, I found my way to the actual factory, sandwiched between rows of redevelopment housing, bulldozers, and cement mixers. The old neighborhood was being torn down in a huge redevelopment movement, and this factory, as my statue maker would later say in the play, was "the last of its kind."

I had made an appointment saying I needed a certain statue. Of course I was prepared to buy a replica of the Virgin Mary if I had to. On my visit the statue maker opened the door ushering me into a world of marble and dust, offering coffee and donuts from an already set table. The message was clear. I had been expected. This was a big deal visit. Once in, he called me by my first name. What did that mean? The situation was sparking a world of possibilities. Anything could happen here … murder, love, fantasy … oh, the excitement of the beginning of things. A play was being born.

In the actual play, it is a high school teacher, Jennie Ames, who comes to find a statue for the class play. Reticent and anxious to leave the factory once she is captive, she becomes more and more uncomfortable with the extended tour, which shows no promise of the statue she has come for, one of Christopher Columbus.

The real situation is always only the beginning. Then the imagination comes into play. You have to decide what will work best for your play, what will make for the greatest tensions and conflicts. So the statue maker in the play became a gentler and older version of the actual sculptor, although he did tell me, regretfully, about the days when people wanted his religious statues, "not just love beads and guitars," which I used directly in the play. Toward the end of the play, Roberto, the sculptor, asks Jennie to stay for dinner, and what a surprise that was to me when I was writing the scene! When you know your characters, they will often write the scene for you. I never did come away with a statue, but I did come away with my first Boston play. The statues for the first production of the play at Brandeis University were supplied by the actual statue maker. Subsequent productions in other cities happily gave renewed business for sculptors of religious statuary.

I was surely surprised during the writing of the play when a rock came flying in through the window of the statue factory. I shouldn't have been. Roberto Da Fralizzi, the statue maker, was hardly startled. "It's the hoodlums," he says. But I had studied the streets outside the actual factory the play was based on, and, as a playwright, I knew what was located in the alleys below. That knowledge allowed that rock to come flying through, even though I hadn't planned it from the start. Location is opportunity.

The confinement of the stage appeals to the playwright, as the freedom to roam is what often attracts the screenwriter. But the genres are not mutually exclusive. The outside always pushes itself into the world of your play.

In a more literal sense, you are never confined to a single set in a play because of location. The first time this was brought home to me was years ago in a production I saw in Sydney, Australia by the aboriginal playwright Billy Marshall Stoneking. The play had six locations. Each had its spot marked out on a small stage, and each was depicted by one or two pieces of furniture. There was an office that was just a simple desk and chair. Then there was a campfire, indicated by a pile of sticks. The bedroom was a single bed. There was a yard denoted by one tree. You get the idea. And so did the audience. Once the locations were established, you always knew where you were. I know this allowed me the freedom to write *A Small Delegation*, a play which took place at the Great Wall of China, the courtyard of the Forbidden City, the Temple of One Hundred Buddhas, a tea room, a passport office, and a banquet hall, all on one stage. Designed by Ming Cho Lee in its initial production at the Annenberg Center in Philadelphia, the innovative set was a series of red tables, arranged according to the changing locations.

Place *is* character. To locate is also to discover the heart of the play, the center of things, and as such, location represents another character. This character has its own history, smell, taste, idiosyncrasies, weaknesses, and strengths.

When I was studying with Israel Horowitz, among the many things he taught me about playwriting and living as a writer was location. The very first thing Israel said was, "Never locate a play in a kitchen or living room. It is boring."

Certainly some of our great plays are set in kitchens, notably Shephard's *Curse of the Starving Class* and its ubiquitous refrigerator. But my teacher wanted us beginning writers to stretch and afford ourselves more breadth. Horowitz has always been a master of situation and location. For his students, now appropriately intimidated, to write a play in a living room or kitchen was to invite disdain. I owe it to Israel that my first play was located in a statue factory, the second, *Exhibition*, took place in the Museum of Modern Art, and another in a casino in Las Vegas. I think it is a lesson that has served me well all my playwriting career, and what has brought me recently to the shores of Marseilles for a location, and next to the streets of South Africa.

As a teacher of playwrights, my travels have taken me all over the world. In helping to set up international programs in writing for New York University's Tisch School of the Arts, and in work for the United States Information Agency, I have encouraged students to use the landscape, to invest, in a way, in the local currency.

In Florence, London, Prague, and South Africa I taught a summer playwriting course with a companion course offered in the history, art, literature, and architecture of that city. Then, the writers were asked to use the city as one of the major locations in their plays.

In London there were stories of the life of Shakespeare, and one in which his ghost returned to witness a production of *The Tempest* at Stratford-on-Avon. There was a murder mystery placed at Oxford, a secretive love affair in the Tower of London, one about the return of a soldier who had been stationed there in World War II who was looking for a lost daughter, and a one-man show about a transvestite from Liverpool who was in love with one of the Beatles. In Prague there were numerous plays about vampires, given one of our excursions to Transylvania, as well as political stories involving the Holocaust and communist years. One play took place inside the old Jewish cemetery in Prague and was about a Dybbuk who haunted it. There was one about a Czech baker with the secret recipe for Easter cakes that was stolen by his main rival in the town.

While I was teaching in Prague, a producer friend Todd Black was filming the movie *A Knight's Tale* there and invited my students to watch some of the filming. Out of it developed a play about a crew from the United States filming in Prague and the conflicts they encountered.

In a class in South Africa, where the students all came from the United States, there were many plays about the apartheid years and the transition to the current government. There was also the play about the Truth and Reconciliation Commission, and the one about the Afrikaner diamond merchant, as well as a play that took place in one of the current townships, Langa, one about the family decimated by AIDS, and a play that took place on the day of Nelson Mandela's inauguration, incorporating his confinement on Robbin Island.

Traveling certainly got these writers out of the kitchen! Passports to playwriting.

A friend recently pointed out that it is astonishing that an inner-city kid like me, brought up in the ghettos of Boston, grew into a writer who absorbed the whole world. Back in those days our world was small, and I had no idea of the places that lay beyond 703 Walkhill Street, and where my journey would take me. All that most of us knew, in that long ago neighborhood, was that we wanted to get out, to go someplace else.

A writer recently confided to me she felt cheated because she had no sense of specific roots. Her father was in the army and she grew up with constantly changing locations. "I have no childhood location to write about," she told me. How can this be true? We all grew up somewhere, and these early images and stories eventually emerge in our plays, transformed by memory, unconsciously or not, as metaphors. These fragments of buried memory are what give our work its specificity, individuality, and location.

This lecture was delivered in Cape Town, South Africa, May 2002, to a group of students in a New York University program abroad titled Writing South Africa. It has been slightly revised for inclusion in the book.

Three Exercises in Location

1. Set up a situation for a scene and write that same scene so it takes place in three different cities. Then take the three scenes you have written and change the set for each one. If one took place in a living room in London, change it to Westminster Bridge. If the next scene is located in the desert of New Mexico, change it to a living room in California. And if the third scene is located in a hotel room in Philadelphia, change it to the compartment of a European train. See how the location affects character and story.

2. If the play you are working on takes place on a one-piece set, consider where else your characters may want to go. Write scenes in these other locations. Does changing location enhance the play and give opportunities for added conflict, as well as raising the stakes? If it does, then consider redesigning your stage concept.

3. Name ten possible locations for a play, either because you have been there or dreamed of going there. You could have the start of a new play. The genesis of a play can be location. I had a hankering to go to Marseilles in my work after I was there, and so was born a play, *After Marseilles*. Character, situation, and plot followed.

7

ENDINGS

When I asked a group of playwrights what the single most difficult task in writing a play was, unanimously they answered, "Endings!" So, I decided to investigate the qualities that combined to formulate a successful ending. I started with the *Oxford English Dictionary*. The definition of an ending is: an action that concludes, completes, or terminates. It is also described as a boundary, an outcome, a result, a final purpose, the object for which the thing exists, the direction in which one wants to play toward, as in the end zone, and, as a destination.[1]

So the ending of a play is the very last image, as well as the very last spoken word. Israel Horowitz instructed his students to note the last word in their play and to determine if there was any significance in that word or sound. Did it connect with the question the play was asking or the conflict it was attempting to resolve?

Playwright John Guare, when asked if he wrote with endings in mind, told an interviewer:

If you knew where you were going why would you bother writing? There'd be nothing to discover. I can still remember throwing up when I realized what the ending of *The House of Blue Leaves* would be — that after Artie the songwriter realized the true worth of his work he would have to kill his wife because she saw him as he was.[2]

In the recent production of Bryony Lavery's play *Last Easter* (2004) off-Broadway at the Lucille Lortel Theatre, the character Gash is played by actor Jeffrey Carlson. He calls after his friend June who has just died from cancer and departed into the "afterlife" by walking down the theater aisle out through the audience, "Is there anything out there?" And he repeats it. It's the final sound of faith being questioned, and because faith is the comic underbelly of this play, the call into the void is all the more wrenching. It completes the journey of the so-called cynical faithless who are, in the last analysis, wanting something after all — call it faith or God, or God spelled backward, as evidenced in the last line of the play, which circles back to the convention of jokes used throughout the play. In this way the author states the case for faith, and at the same time questions it. What is remarkable about the ending is how it sneaks up on you. The play appears to be a comedy about a group of friends supporting a friend through her last days of cancer, but it turns ever so gently at the end, kicking you in the heart, and it is a wipeout.

In examining endings, we should look to fairytales as models. In the fairytale there is generally a problem that has to be solved, whether it is the wolf that has devoured Little Red Riding Hood's grandmother or Sleeping Beauty who can only be woken by a kiss from a Prince. When that problem, or the evil, is confronted, the story can come to its conclusion, which means a change of circumstances and therefore, closure.

Peter Brooks, in his book *Readings for the Plot*, states that narrative is one of the ways in which we think and speak, and "plot is its thread of design and active shaping force, the product of our refusal to allow temporality to be meaningless, our stubborn insistence on making meaning in the world and in our lives."[3] So it is in our endings where we find the meaning in our plays, and this meaning shows its face to the writer only at the completion of the journey of writing.

Arthur Miller, in his essay on "The Family in Modern Drama," says that it is content which dictates form, and so no rules about endings can be applied mechanically. For me, this is a central joy in writing a play — figuring out the individual architecture for each piece. In the same essay, Miller says:

> Most people, including the daily theater reviewers, have come to assume that the forms in which plays are written, spring either from nowhere or from the temperamental choice of the playwrights. I am not maintaining that the selection of the form is as objective a matter as the choice of let us say a raincoat instead of a linen suit for a walk on a rainy day; on the contrary, most playwrights, including myself, reach rather instinctively for that form, that telling of a play, which seems inevitably right for the subject at hand.[4]

And so it is with endings.

When you are coming to the conclusion of your play, you are a chariot driver with many reins in your two hands; and, as you are nearing the finish of the race, you are holding on tighter and tighter to these reins, so that they all knot into one.

What are these reins? You are holding in your hands all the narrative threads of your play. When we speak about a playwright "earning an ending" we mean that the ending should be organic to the narrative line of the play.

Sometimes I go back over a play and first diagram the narrative lines for each character. Then I diagram the accompanying emotional lines for each character. Next I diagram the action of the play from beginning to end. Then I return to the original question the play is asking and see if the through-line of that question manifests itself in the script.

When these complex threads are outlined, I put them up on a wall or down on a flat surface so I can review the scope of the play. Then I commit these various threads to memory and walk with them for a while. You want to make certain that you as a playwright have followed through on all the lines of your play. Now, holding these lines as reins, as a chariot driver, draw them tighter and tighter to your chest until the concluding image is forged between your two hands. Many times, this final image just comes to you when you are doing something else — walking in the park, taking a shower, or eating ice cream. This image evolves seemingly mysteriously, but it works its way out of the subconscious much as a baby chick breaking out of an egg.

Now, we should examine some endings of plays in order to see what works effectively in a drama.

In Conor McPherson's new play *Shining City*, which opened at the Royal Court Theater in London in the summer of 2004 and takes place in Dublin, a man comes to a therapist seeking help. He claims to have seen the ghost of his recently deceased wife.

> I was just going into the living room and I put the lights on, and … when I turned around I could see that she was standing there behind the door looking at me … her hair was soaking wet, and all plastered to her face … I mean it's unbelievable, you know … well finally, I don't know how, but I just got my legs going and went straight out the door, straight by her … she was behind it.[5]

The man describes the ghost of his wife as being dressed in red. In the course of the play, the therapist "cures" the man, taking his red-dressed ghost away from him. The therapist has his own problems, which his patient "outs." The following are the final moments of the play. The therapist is Ian, and his patient, now cured, is John.

Ian: I think you had a real experience. I think you really experienced something — but I think it happened because you needed to experience it ... you
were pulling all this ... you felt maybe you couldn't
move on without being ... punished somehow ... it
happened! BUT ... I don't believe you saw a ghost.
Does that make sense?

John: Well, yeah, it makes sense to me now. But there was
a time it really wouldn't have, you know? But that
was a different time.

Ian: Yeah, it was.

John: ... I'll see you.

Ian: I'll wait here till you get out down there.

John: I'll see you Ian, good luck.

Ian: I'll see you, John, bye now.

(*Ian hovers near the open door while John goes down. We hear
the outer door slam shut. Ian calls out*)

Ian: Did you get out?

(*There is no answer. Ian shuts the door and crosses the room.
In the darkening gloom of the afternoon, we see that the ghost
of John's wife has appeared behind the door. She is looking
at Ian, just as John described her; she wears her red coat and
her hair is wet. She looks terrifying. Ian has his back to her
at his desk, going through some papers. But he seems to sense
something and turns.*)

(*Lights down.*)[6]

In this drama, two men help each other in a desperate struggle
between the living and the dead. One goes off cured, as he hoped,
and the other inherits the ghost in red.

Lorraine Hansberry's *A Raisin in the Sun* refers to a Langston
Hughes poem, "Harlem."

What happens to a dream deferred?
Does it dry up
Like a raisin in the sun?
Or fester like a sore –
And then run?
Does it stink like rotten meat
Or crust and sugar over –
Like a syrupy sweet?

Maybe it just sags
Like a heavy load.

Or does it explode?[7]

In *A Raisin in the Sun*, the Younger family, a struggling black family living in Chicago in the 1950s, inherits $10,000 in insurance money from their deceased father and decides to purchase a house in a white neighborhood. As the family packs, a representative from the neighborhood, Carl Lindner, comes with a proposal: the Clybourne Park Neighborhood Association will pay the Youngers *not* to move in. The family refuses. However, when Walter Lee, the supposed head of the household, loses $6,500 of the insurance money in a venture to open a liquor store, he says he will allow the family to be bought out. He says, "You know it's all divided up. Life is. Sure enough. Between the takers and the 'tooken."[8]

Walter Lee is tired of falling into the latter category. His sister, Beneatha, swears that if he kneels to the powers that be, he will no longer be her brother, and their mother, Lena (the *actual* head of the household), chastises Beneatha:

Child, when do you think is the time to love somebody the most? When they done good and made things easy for everybody? ... That ain't the time at all. It's when he's at his lowest and can't believe in hisself 'cause the world done whipped him so![9]

Soon after that, Lindner arrives again, ready to pay the Youngers off; however, Walter Lee defies everyone's expectations, saying:

> We have decided to move into our house because my fa-
> ther — my father — he earned it for us brick by brick.
> We don't want to make no trouble for nobody or fight no
> causes, and we will try to be good neighbors. And that's *all*
> we got to say about that. We don't want your money.[10]

As soon as Mr. Lindner is gone, the family returns quickly to the frenzy of moving, attempting to ignore the nobility of Walter's action. After everyone is gone, we see Mama, alone in the apartment she's raised her children in:

> *Mama stands, at last alone in the living room, her plant on*
> *the table before her as the lights start to come down. She looks*
> *around at all the walls and ceilings and suddenly, despite her-*
> *self, while the children call below, a great heaving thing rises*
> *in her and she puts her fist to her mouth to stifle it, takes a*
> *final desperate look, pulls her coat about her, pats her hat and*
> *goes out. The lights dim down. The door opens and she comes*
> *back in, grabs her plant, and goes out for the last time.*[11]

The final moment of the play with Mama encapsulates the struggle of the mother for acceptance of her family's place in society, and the family's defiance of the housing restrictions, threats, and bribery, all meant to keep the present social order intact. Lorraine Hansberry, relating the lessons her parents taught her that later influenced the play, says in the introduction, "We were the products of the proudest and most mistreated of the races of men ... above all, there were two things which were never to be betrayed, the family and the race." The play is dedicated, "To Mama: *in gratitude for the dream.*"

The play is about the quest for a dream. The Youngers do get their dream. They will move to the house in the all-white neighborhood. But there is a price for that acquisition and for their disruption of the status quo. A *Raisin in the Sun* premiered on Broadway in 1959, in the midst of the civil rights movement, and as such, represents choices that had to be made by an entire generation. The play, although highly personal, relates to the entirety of the 1960s and civil liberties. The Youngers' fight became everybody's fight. The dreams of the civil rights movement were not achieved without a cost. Mama is all of us, trying to get out.

What does Hansberry accomplish with the silence of the play's final moment? One interpretation is that Mama stares the future in the face, knows it is uncertain; she owns both the victory and the knowledge of the struggle ahead. She takes one last look around her house, gets dressed in her armor of coat and hat, opens the door, doesn't slam it, and comes back in at the last minute to grab her plant. She is taking both the remnants of the past and the possibility of growth in the future.

In Wendy Wasserstein's *The Sisters Rosensweig* — a different kind of family play — we watch three Jewish women from Brooklyn gather at the eldest's house in Queen Anne's Gate, London. They all have strayed far from their roots, though the middle daughter, Gorgeous, has done basically what was expected of her: she married a lawyer, had kids, moved to the suburbs of Boston, and is leading the women's group from her synagogue on a tour of London. The play deals with the complex relationship between what these women are looking for and what they actually have, as well as their distance from each other and their past. The play opens with Tess, the eldest sister Sara's daughter, listening to a recording of her mother's a cappella group from college; she's doing a biography of her mother's early years for a school project. "It's pretentious," Tess says as the play begins. Though singing was clearly an important part of Sara's past, she refuses to sing throughout the play, until its closing moments. Gorgeous has just left to return the Chanel ensemble the women's group has given her as a thank-you gift so she can pay her children's tuition; Pfeni

(the youngest) has gone to Tajikistan to write the book she's always meant to; and Sara has just said goodbye (maybe temporarily,
maybe not) to the new, older, and very sensible man in her life.
Finally alone with her mom, Tess asks Sara for an interview for
her school project.

Sara: My name is Sara Rosensweig. I am the daugh-
            ter of Rita and Maury Rosensweig. I was born in
            Brooklyn, New York, August 23, 1937.
Tess: And when did you first sing?
Sara: I made my debut at La Scala at fourteen.
Tess: Mother!
Sara: I first sang at the Hanukah Festival at East
            Midwood Jewish Center. I played a candle.
Tess: And why did you become a Cliffe Clef?
Sara: Your great-grandfather thought I could be a singer.
Tess: Would you sing something now?
Sara: Honey, it's so early.
Tess: Please sing something. (*Begins to sing.*)
            Shine on, shine on, harvest moon
            Up in the sky.
Sara: I ain't had no loving since January, February, June, or
            July.
Tess: Do it, mother!
Sara: Snow time ain't no time to stay outdoors and spoon.
Tess and Sara: So shine on, shine on, harvest moon.
Sara: (*Sings, touching her daughter's face*) For me and my
            gal.[12,13]

In this simple gesture, we see, finally, a hard-won moment of
pure connection between mother and daughter, past and present.
While we know that these characters will continue to struggle, a
small understanding and a fragile bond has been accomplished.

The Sisters Rosensweig owes a great deal to Chekhov's *The Three Sisters*. Its ending, however, doesn't leave us with the same tender glow. Olga, Masha, and Irina spend the entire play looking for a way to escape their provincial existence and return to their hometown, Moscow. Like Sara, Gorgeous, and Pfeni, they are living in a present in which all connections to their past have disappeared. Unlike the sisters Rosensweig, these women are not trying to escape their past, but rather return to it. When the handsome captain Vershinin comes to town and they realize that they knew him in Moscow, he immediately becomes a constant guest in their home — and inspires vivid dreams of a return to the city. However, as it often is in Chekhov's stories and in life, nothing goes according to plan. By the end of the fourth act, Irina's fiancé, Tuzenbach, has been shot in a duel, all the soldiers, including Vershinin, are leaving, and Natasha, their sister-in-law, has declared that their favorite orchard of cherry trees, outside the family home, will be cut down to make way for new housing. After the discovery of Tuzenbach's death, the sisters are left alone with the retired army doctor, Chebutykin. They listen to the music of the departing soldiers.

Masha: Listen, how the music is playing! They are going away from us, one of them has already gone, gone forever, and we are left here alone to start our lives again. We must go on living... We must go on living...

Irina: (*Leans her head on Olga's breast.*) The time will come, and everyone will know the meaning of all this, why there is all this suffering, and there won't be any mysteries, but meanwhile, we must go on living... we must work, we must work! Tomorrow I will leave on my own, I will teach in a school and I'll give all my life to those perhaps who need it. It's already autumn, soon it will be winter, the snow will fall, but I will be working, I will go on working...

Olga: (*Embraces both sisters.*) The music is playing so cheerfully, it's so full of high spirits that one wants to stay alive. Oh God, Oh God! The time will come when we will be gone forever, we will be forgotten, our faces, our voices, and even how many of us there were. But our suffering will be transformed into happiness for those who live after us, peace and contentment will cover the earth, and they will remember and bless with kind words all those who live now. My dearest, dearest sisters, our life is still not finished. We will go on living. The music is playing so happily, so cheerfully, that it seems, in just a little time, we will know why we live, and why there is all this suffering... If only we could know! If only we could know!

(*The music becomes quieter and quieter; Kulygin, smiling and happy, Masha's hat and shawl; Andrey wheels out the pram with Bobik sitting in it.*)

Chebutykin: (*Sings quietly.*) Ta-ra-ra boom-de-boom, I sat upon a stone... (Reads the paper.) It doesn't matter! It doesn't matter!

Olga: If only we could know! If only we could know!

CURTAIN[14]

Even as the sister's hope of change in their situation ebbs away, they are resolved to continue their lives as they have always lived them. This is the only certainty they have. As the music continues to fade, however, Olga can only lament the blindness with which they must make their way through life; working without any proof of reward. Everything and nothing has changed, the past remains inaccessible, and the future is without promise. The action of the play is the raising of hopes and the crushing of them. The resolution is a coming to terms with reality, at least for one of the sisters — Olga.

In Caryl Churchill's *Far Away*, a young girl has come to live with her aunt and can't sleep because she has witnessed some horrors on the property. The young girl questions her aunt about seeing her uncle hitting people with an iron bar. The young girl, Joan, had climbed out of bed and into a tree in the yard where she witnessed the uncle bundling someone into the shed, and then witnessed children in the shed with blood on their faces. The aunt at first denies it, saying Joan saw things she shouldn't have and then admits that one of the people the uncle was hitting was found to be a traitor, and that the whole family will now be on the side of right, fighting the traitors. "You're part of a big movement now to make things better," says the aunt to the child. So the first scene is one of a world we don't recognize, but in a larger sense, we do, and it is one filled with violence and portends worse. When I saw the first scene I was reminded of China in the days preceding Tiananmen Square. There was something "bad" in the air.

By the end of the play, and several years later, the entire world is at war, chained prisoners march on their way to execution, and Joan returns to her aunt's house and describes her journey on the way.

Joan: There were piles of bodies, and if you stopped to
            find out there was one killed by coffee, or one killed
            by pins, they were killed by heroin, petrol, chain-
            saws, hairspray, bleach, foxgloves, the smell of smoke
            was where we were burning the grass that wouldn't
            serve. ... There was a camp of Chilean soldiers
            upstream but they hadn't seen me and fourteen
            black and white cows downstream having a drink
            so I knew I'd have to go straight across. But I didn't
            know whose side the river was on, it might help me
            swim or it might drown me. In the middle the cur-
            rent was running much faster, the water was brown,
            I didn't know if that meant anything. I stood on the

bank a long time. But I knew it was my only way of getting here so at last I put one foot in the river. It was very cold but so far that was all. When you've just stepped in you can't tell what's going to happen. The water laps round your ankles in any case.[15]

The play begins in a world on the verge of going awry and ends with a world gone completely out of control and one where there is little hope for respite. Only the most insignificant physical facts can be counted on.

Churchill is reminding us from the play's very start, in which someone is pushing someone into a shed, through the Parade of the Hats, led by a procession of ragged, beaten, and chained prisoners on their way to execution, that we are all dehumanized. Churchill leaves us with the image of devastation as witnessed by a young girl and shows us the innocence and strength with which she faces adversity. At the beginning of the play, Joan is at her Aunt Harper's house and can't sleep. By the end of the play, Harper warns Joan, "You can't stay here, they'll be after you, they'll be after you" and Joan is trying to escape through the mountains, through "rats bleeding out of their mouths and ears," and past the dead bodies. It's not certain how far away she can get from this world.

Sam Shepard's *Curse of the Starving Class* tells the story of a family in rural California. No one in the family is physically starving, but they are hungry for identity and selfhood, for roots, and for status. The journey of the play is a quest for self-esteem and a larger place in the universe. Nobody gets that, but one member of the family, Wesley, sees that his only choice is to give up the dream and cling to the roots he already has. The family is torn apart by the very thing that binds them together: their desire to escape their lower-middle-class lives. They want something better for themselves, but they don't know where that is or how to get there. There is an emptiness that they can't fill. This is symbolized

on stage by their refrigerator, which they are continually opening, staring into, and, finding nothing to their liking, slamming
shut. Ella says to Wesley, "How can you be hungry all the time?
We're not poor. We're not rich but we're not poor." Wesley replies,
"What are we then?" The action of the play is the family trying to
find this out. Ella promises that they're going to have some money
real soon, and then their lives will change. Their search is not unlike that of the Youngers in *A Raisin in the Sun* or Chekhov's *Three
Sisters*.

In the course of the play, the father, Weston, is constantly bor-
rowing money for things he can't afford: land in the desert, liquor,
and cars. His wife, Ella, threatens to sell their house and head for
Europe. Their daughter, Emma, threatens to take the horse and
run away to Mexico. Only the son, Wesley, has resisted the family's
self-destruction. By the play's end, however, he too has lost hope,
putting on his father's discarded, dirty clothes. By this point, Ella
has passed out on the kitchen table, and Weston has presumably
left home to avoid the bill collectors. Emma has taken the keys
to her mother's car and is about to start a journey of her own.
Ella wakes screaming just as her daughter is leaving. Suddenly,
there is an explosion outside that rocks the house. The bill collectors, Emerson and Slater, have arrived. They enter, giggling,
and when Wesley asks what blew up, they say, "Something that
wasn't paid for. Something past due." They have blown up the car,
and Emerson says, "Well, that's what comes from not paying your
bills."[16]

The final image of the play is of an eagle and a cat locked
in a struggle that neither can win. This is the end of a story that
Weston had begun earlier, in which he feeds lamb testicles to a
soaring eagle. Ella and Wesley stand perfectly still, facing in opposite directions. Ella finishes the story, picking up where her husband left off.

Ella: They fight like crazy in the middle of the sky. That
             cat's tearing his chest out, and the eagle's trying to
             drop him, but the cat won't let go because he knows
             if he falls he'll die.
Wesley: And the eagle's being torn apart in midair. The
             eagle's trying to free himself from the cat, and the
             cat won't let go.
Ella: And they come crashing down to the earth. Both of
             them come crashing down. Like one whole thing.[17]

The image of this cursed family is echoed in the representation of the eagle and the cat. They are in a struggle, which results
in the absence of the father, and the death of the daughter. The
mother and son are left, witnessing the devastation, part of the
same cursed entity, but never really connecting.

We have looked at a variety of effective endings, but it's impossible to know the process by which their authors reached them.
I would suggest reading playwright's letters and biographies when
available and trying to gain insight into their methods and intentions. I would particularly recommend *Playwrights at Work*[18] and
Playwrights in Rehearsal.[19] I can, however, address some of my own
plays and the processes I used to forge my endings.

In my one-act play *The Bridge at Belharbour*, a suburban wid-
ow, Valerie Marino, emerges as something of an angel of death.
She has called a plumber, Tom Fahey, to her house overlooking
the Atlantic, to clear her stopped-up drain. There is an obvious
class difference between the woman and the plumber, and she is
anxious to mine that difference for all it's worth, assaulting the
plumber's dignity. In the course of the one-hour play, played in real
time, she manages to elicit enough information about the plumber
to discover all his vulnerabilities. Every stated truth in the play is
conditional and problematical and shaped by forces crouching just
out of view.

Midway through the play, Valerie flirts with Tom:

Valerie: You've been watching me, haven't you, out of the
              corner of your eyes. Don't be afraid.
Tom: I ain't.

But shortly after, when Tom succumbs to her obvious gesture toward him and goes to kiss her movie star fashion (which is the best he can summon up), she pulls away in disgust. This is the beginning of the end for Tom. Valerie, from the beginning, has set out to destroy this stranger, out of a kind of misplaced retaliation for her own miseries.

Tom: What do you think I am? Some dumb slob you can
              cast off like a fly. You can't fool around with people
              like that. I shouldn't have done that ... you made
              me.
Valerie: I didn't make you do anything. ... Oh, go home, why
              don't you, home to your wife and your seven ugly
              kids and your above ground swimming pool and the
              big holes in your mouth where your teeth fell out
              and you haven't got the money to replace them. I
              saw. I saw when your mouth was open.[20]

And this is only the beginning of the assault. By the end of the play, Valerie has succeeded in crushing what small ego Tom has, and the end suggests Tom's planned suicide on the way home. (This was an ending I did not plan but evolved in the writing of the play.) This same suicide, off the bridge at Belharbour, echoes Valerie's reverie about the same bridge, and how some days it is just waiting for her and she would like to fly off of it, like some bird.

Valerie: The leaves are blowing upside down.
Tom: Heat's gonna break.

Valerie: It's started to rain. Maybe you ought to leave before
             the storm gets too bad.
Tom: Yeah, I'd better get moving.
Valerie: Maybe you shouldn't take the shore road.
Tom: Yeah. I'm real tired.
Valerie: Perhaps you ought to use the new highway instead.
Tom: By way of that bridge you was talkin' about before.
Valerie: What bridge?
Tom: The one you said they built just for you.
Valerie: For me?
Tom: You said …
Valerie: You hear what you want to hear, Mr. Fahey.
Tom: No. You said the bridge at Belharbour is waiting …
             (*Valerie shrugs her shoulders*)[21]
Tom: Well guess I'd better be going. Sorry I never got the
             sink unplugged.
Valerie: I'll find someone else.

He then leaves the opals he had bought for his wife as a birthday
present, which Valerie had pronounced to be bad luck.

Valerie: Don't forget the opals.
Tom: Keep 'em. I don't want them.
Valerie: You sure?
Tom: I'm sure … well so long … and good luck to you.
Valerie: I already used up my good luck.
Tom: Nah, I don't think so. Goodbye Mrs. Marino
(*Tom exits*)
Valerie: I'm sorry, but everyone has to live. It's such a
             crowded planet.[22]

At this point, with Tom gone, she chillingly takes out the
package with the opals in it, unwraps it, and puts on the opal neck-
lace. Valerie is an even match for Hedda Gabler. What I always

liked about the ending of *The Bridge at Belharbour* is the spare of language that echoes the silence of death. It's in the sounds and the rhythms. All I can remember of the writing of it is the utter quietude and slow, steady march to the end. At that moment all the reins were in my hands.

In writing the end of a recent play, *After Marseilles*, I began by rereading what I had written so far, and then reviewed all the notes I had made on the play, culled from a reading at the O'Neill Theatre Center, a reading at Primary Stages in New York, from colleagues and audiences for the readings, and my own comments and clarifications.

After Marseilles was begun on the eve of the millennium. Looking back at history, it seemed to me more and more marked by random acts of violence, and then, less randomly: greed, ambition, and the erosion of the environment and public trust. We were becoming a world without a moral backbone. Our focus had been accumulation and power, and we seemed like a runaway train, heading for disaster.

What if, I thought, we were forced to live with a disaster of our own making, or, because of natural forces or a combination; how would we re-create a new world?

The play opens in a world that has been destroyed by a natural catastrophe. It is the end of civilization as we know it. Five characters — Sam, Dakota, Zoe, Chip, and Madame Zaza — are blown onto the rocky coast of Marseilles, much the same as Odysseus was driven onto the coast of a strange land. In the face of government intimidation, and led by Madame Zaza, a native of Paris and a clothes designer, they try to rebuild.

Because we write to find out what it is we are writing about, it is not until three-quarters through and usually the second draft, at least, that we begin to understand the full complexity of what we're working on and the questions it's asking. In addition, if we have done our homework and conceived biographies for all the characters and worked out the back-story, encompassing that time the characters spent before they all walked into your play, some of the characters will start to take us in a direction we couldn't have possibly conceived in any outline. You have to trust that. If you listen to your characters they will tell you what their deepest desires are, and you will understand what they are trying to get in the play and what is standing in their way.

The following are some excerpts from the hundreds of pages of notes I made while writing the first four drafts of *After Marseilles*. They are the major comments I used in order to write the end of the play. Since Madame Zaza is the major character, it was her journey I was concentrating on. I was looking for hints in my notes and in her lines in the play.

- Zaza is doing everything she does in order to prevent herself from dying ... dealing with the waning of her life.
- What are Zaza's honest emotions at every moment in the play?
- Zaza realizes in the end she is doomed to mortality.
- To stop death in its tracks one has to look for meaning in the present.
- Tragedy shows us the best and worst of human beings.
- How to have the courage of your own life in an age without morality or reason.
- Is there reason in an unreasonable universe?
- Let Zaza reveal herself through an action.
- On the Day of Atonement it is written in "The Book," who shall die and who shall live that year. Zaza sees her name written in the book.
- There is a longing to go back to America. Many Americans thought they wanted a European kind of sophistication, but now want community and their own roots.

- Make everyone's yearnings real so their disappointments can be real.
- As long as the other characters stay, Zaza has a purpose.
- How do we get from destruction to possibility?
- "This has been the bloodiest century in the history of the human race." (From an editorial in the *New York Times* by James Reston, May 30, 1982)
- A small act of love redeems the characters.
- In the blues the human spirit is acknowledging both pain and soaring.
- Is Zaza a fool or a prophet?
- What pushes the play forward is Zaza's desire to live, to continue in the face of hopelessness.
- I think of the future as stretching forward before me and I go forward to meet it.
- Man takes a positive hand whenever he puts a building in the earth beneath the sun.
- To overcome our feelings of hopelessness and channel our rage and anguish toward "constructive ends." (From an editorial in the *New York Times*, October 2002 titled "Betraying Humanity" by Bob Herbert)
- Stakes are what characters have to win or lose.
- What is it that shatters Zaza's spirit? When she is found out to be lying? When she realizes she has to let everyone go and face her own death alone?
- What does Zaza want? To hold on to her life spirit and to never give up. To be in control.
- What I love about Zaza — she has the courage of her own life. She is a celebrant. She does not want to leave life, and so her reluctance to let it all go … but she cannot keep back the tides.

At one moment, when I was nearing the end of one of the drafts of the play and was seated at a desk overlooking the ocean,

I got a strong feeling that Zaza was trying to hold back the ocean from rolling, to stop the inevitable tides. It was this strong pull and image that ultimately gave me the end of my play and contributed to the note, above, about holding back the ocean.

This moment with *After Marseilles* and Zaza was the one in which I truly discovered that we write to learn what it is we are writing about. Some of the play was originally conceived from a *New York Times* article about this century being the bloodiest in history. That editorial was from 1982, but it was not until 2000, that I would revisit the article and start the play. I had recently visited Marseilles and found it to be a kind of crossroads of the world. It occurred to me that if the world ever ended, this is where it would end, at the tip of France, where Europe connects to Africa. And I was off!

I know, as a teacher of playwrights, that an outline should be required at the start; but, to be honest, I have never followed a complete outline, for the very reason stated above — that we write to find out our subject. In addition, the character work at some point, if it is done in depth, takes over, and the characters lead us out of their desires. I often ask for an outline, but know that it will never be completely followed. It is meant as a blueprint to get started and to see where you think you are going.

So I began *After Marseilles* thinking it was a play about the aftermath of a catastrophe and how a group of people would rebuild. I knew that Madame Zaza, the leader, took her orders from Paris, but only as I continued writing did I realize she had a large secret; she was making up a fictitious government in Paris and improvising all the rules. There was no government. Zaza was fashioning order to prevent chaos.

That image of Zaza trying to hold back the ocean is one of those electrifying moments that are the absolute joy of being a playwright. You see, our work is to solve problems, and here the answer was on a golden platter. I understood the metaphor perfectly. Zaza wanted to hold on to life, to hold back her own mortality. And it came out of her very love of life. I did recognize my own feelings, subconscious as they were. I was on the other side of fifty now, and I didn't know exactly how I'd gotten there, but I wanted this aging to stop! If only I could only hold back the tides. That was Zaza's secret and she held it from me until the second draft. It came to me at the O'Neill Theatre Center, sitting at my desk, looking out onto the Atlantic and the waves rolling in and back.

Here are the last pages of *After Marseilles*:

> (*Sam enters carrying two pieces of luggage*)

Sam: They found it! They found your luggage. It arrived this morning,

> (*The sounds of a bird, low pitched, grating, loud, insistent, like wagon wheels across bricks*)

Zoe: What's that?

Sam: Fork-tailed drongo. It has a low, mournful sound, like "whoo whee" ... listen.

> (*Repeated sound of bird*)

It warns all the other animals that danger's near. It smells it before it appears. In the bush, to the south, it warns the smaller animals of predators, of leopards or lions. That's his sound. I know it.

> (*Zaza gets up from the table, returns to the shop she's building, hammering up more boards. The bird continues to call. The sky becomes darker.*)

Sam: Something's coming over the bridge, from the south, with the storm. Far away, but you can hear ... packs of hyenas, lions, herds of elephants, buffalo, and rhino.

Dakota: How do you know?

> (*During the following exchange it starts to rain, light at first, then harder*)

Sam: My grandmother taught me birds and animals; she taught me to listen. She believed all animals were sacred. The drongo is warning the littlest ones, the young cubs, the impalas, that a leopard is coming, walking alone. The leopards are the holiest and the fiercest, and always unaccompanied. They're likely coming from the Kruger, or from the Serengeti, even as far as the Cape of Good Hope. I can never be sure what I'm hearing, but I feel it. We should leave. It's time to go.

Chip: To where?

Zaza: You could try west, on foot, up through the Pyrenees, or north through the Alps. Go. Hurry up!

Dakota: Then come on. Let's get going, Zaza.

Zaza: I'm not coming.

Dakota: What do you mean?

Zaza: No. I need to finish building my shop. My heart's set on it.

(*They all just stand there.*)

Go ahead! Go! Get out of here! And don't feel badly for me. I lived the life I wanted.

(*They all remain standing. The rain continues. Sound of animals is nearer.*)

Move. Go! One, two, three, one, two, three ...
You too, Sam.

(*They start leaving, but in the opposite direction of the bridge that supposedly connects to Africa. They leave behind the found luggage. Then they stop, hesitate, look back for a moment at Zaza.*)

Zaza: In Spain, you know, there are oranges on the trees.

Sam (*to Zaza*): Let us know you got home safely.

Zaza: I will. And who knows? After Marseilles? Maybe there's something better ... or something.

(They exit, disappearing, as if into light, leaving Zaza
alone on the stage, hammering away at her new shop.
The rain stops. The wind dies down. Sound of the bird.)

THE END[23]

In rereading the end of the play, it is interesting that *The Bridge at Belharbour*, an early play, and *After Marseilles*, a much later play, both end with weather. And yet, I cannot think of another play I have written that ends with weather. There is, however, a shared element in both play endings; they both reflect a probable death for one of the characters. I think it is simulated in the rhythm of the rising storm and the subsequent silence at the very close of the play.

The last scene, called "Le Banquet Finale" takes place at a celebratory banquet, heralding the end of a long famine, except that all the food has been stolen. Madame Zaza, prior to the banquet, has been building a dress shop to replace the elegant one she once owned in Paris. As part of the set, there is also a bridge that is rumored to go to Africa. Other than Madame Zaza, the other four are from the United States, or what used to be the United States, and there is hardly a chance they are going to ever make it anywhere, once they decide to leave. But they are going to try. It also came as a surprise that Madame Zaza was not going with them and they reluctantly leave her behind in the end.

So how did I come to these choices? Well, first, the image of animals coming two by two, from Africa, and over the bridge, came to me. The representation, obviously, is from the flood in the Bible, signaling terrible times coming. But these animals, rather than entering the safety of an ark, are raging wildly, and together with the mournful call of the bird, constitute an ominous force, and therefore give way to a hurried departure.

Once that final moment came to me, it was clear, that Zaza would choose to stay, ready now to face the very mortality she has been trying to avoid. Also, she would finally let go of the others, realizing that she has to be alone in order to let go, or die. I then remembered a friend who had suffered a long illness, saying, at the last, not to feel pity for her as she had lived the very life she wanted. That was a gift to give a friend, and a line that always had, for me, resonance, clarity, dignity and grace. I love being able to use it for Zaza because in the courrse of the play she comes to a similar recognition and owns her biogrpahy.

In addition, I remembered a guide I met in South Africa who related how his father taught him the meanings of animal sounds and particularly those of African birds. When this guide was trying to locate a leopard in the bush, for example he looked to the flight direction and sounds of some of those birds. He told me the birds warned the other animals of the leopard's approach, as well as weather patterns. It was said that this guide was the only one who could always locate the elusive and solitary leopard, as well as impending storms.

I cannot tell you where the line "In Spain, you know, there are oranges on the trees," came from, but, I did not want to directly say they would be going home through Spain. So the above was a way of articulating the idea of hope and oranges growing on trees. When Sam tells Zaza to let them know when she gets home safely, he is, of course, referring to some kind of afterlife.

What astonishes the playwright in writing an ending is how you could not have possibly known it in the beginning. By the time you come to the end, you know the characters so well and their journey, they are truly, like all good characters, writing the very lines for you.

This is some of what I know about writing an ending.

This lecture was delivered to a group of Advanced Playwriting Students, New York's University's Tisch School of the Arts, Goldberg Department of Dramatic Writing, Fall 2004. It has been slightly revised for inclusion in this book.

Three Exercises in Writing Endings

1. Look at the endings to Tennessee Williams's *The Glass Menagerie*, *A Streetcar Named Desire*, and *Cat on a Hot Tin Roof*. Then go back and trace the themes in the three plays, analyzing how the author came to those endings and what those endings accomplish.

2. For the same three plays, what three different endings could you construct and how would that change the meaning of the plays?

3. Write a poem based on something you feel passionately about. Then take the last line and write it as a last scene in a play, fashioning the back story based on the rest of your poem. Is it possible you may have the idea for a new play here?

8
REWRITING

When the Department of Playwriting at NYU's Tisch School of the Arts was founded, it was called simply the Dramatic Writing Program. Often, I called it the Dramatic *Re*writing Program. It's hard to accept the fact that we are only beginning our journey with a play when we finish the first draft. In order to face the series of rewrites a play requires, I think it best to approach the task in a formulaic way, so that you have a predetermined set of steps to go through and don't feel overwhelmed. In rewriting a play, I make a list of problems I want to tackle and attack one task at a time. For example, if I have to deepen one character's voice, I work on that throughout the script from beginning to end. Then, if I have some plot difficulties, I reshuffle the plot so that it all flows together. Don't attack all your problems at the same time. List them, and vanquish them one at a time.

In order to create a hands-on outline for all rewrites, I did three things:

1. Made a list of possible problems to deal with in a rewrite.

2. Did interviews about the rewriting process with fiction writers, nonfiction writers, playwrights, and poets.

3. Compiled examples of rewritten pages from playwright's scripts.

Common Problems to Be Solved in a Rewrite and Suggested Exercises

Strengthen One Character's Voice:

Suggestion: If you haven't yet found your character's voice (and you will know because all that character's speeches are generic rather than individualized), then ask your character a central question about his or her childhood or mother, and have the character answer in his or her own voice. You will absolutely find the character's voice this way, providing you write it honestly and from the character's point of view, and not your own as the playwright.

Deepen Characterization:

Suggestion: If you find one of your characters lacks complexity, first, look up the word "complex" in the dictionary. The *Oxford English Dictionary* defines it as "integrate, or something that is not easily analyzed or disentangled." A complex character should have many opposing parts in his or her personality that encompass both their Apollonian and Dionysian aspects.

In order to create a more complex character, I also ask my character a question in his or her own voice — but a question that involves his or her ethical standards.

The Plot Is Not Complex Enough and Lacks a Large Enough Conflict to Lead to a Dramatic Incident:

Suggestion: Read the Bible, the storylines of operas, or the daily newspaper or weekly news magazine in order to get ideas about plot complications. But the bottom line is this: the complications of a plot are based on what the central character *wants* and just how far he or she will go to get it. So, go back and ask that question of your protagonist: "What do you really want? What will you do to get it?"

Editing:

Your play is hugely overwritten. How do you know? First, your pages are thick with language and have very little "air." Second, there are interchanges that, though pleasant and real, do not further plot or characterization.

Suggestions: Go through every single phrase, line, and speech, and see what you can lose. If something is not the result of previous action, or the cause of future action, or illuminating to characterization, it's unnecessary.

If the play is simply conversational (no matter how clever) or marking time and not moving forward, see where you can make a large cut while maintaining the sense of the whole. In a rewrite, you must be able to kill your darlings.

Next, go through every long speech and see if it is really intrinsic to the script, or if it is you the playwright who is speaking. Next, see how many sentences and phrases you can lose from within the speech to make it shorter and sharper.

When you have completed your first round of editing, go back to the beginning and do it *again*. This editing process will continue through workshops and rehearsals, until the play is tight and clean as you can make it. I have never reread a script, or been in a reading, workshop, or rehearsal for full production where I did not cut lines and improve the play.

Missing Emotional Moments:

Sometimes, instead of writing too much, we underwrite, and a large recognition and reversal is done in one or two lines. Often, we need more steps going toward the moment of climax. Since it is not mathematical, no one can tell you how many; it is more like a piece of music or a poem, in that you will know when it is just right.

Suggestion: Improvise specific moments with an actor and you will often get your answer. I use this method in class when a playwright is having difficulty realizing the depth of an emotional moment. We improvise right on the spot, often having exhanges between two or three sets of people, until we find it.

Individuation of Voices:

Sometimes we get two characters speaking in the same voice. This is simply a matter of redoing your biographical homework.

Suggestion: First, decide which character the doubled voice will belong to. Then, draw up a new set of biographical questions to ask the other character, and interview him or her, asking leading questions, and then redo every speech belonging to that character. It's important to take on the physical and emotional complexities of your character during every speech so he or she is reacting anew. Be warned that this may change the plot, but it will certainly make for a more honest play.

Lack of Clarity:

In other words, no one understands what your play is about, or they understand too late.

Suggestion: Go back to the major conflict of the play. Ask yourself why you wanted to write this play and what it is basically about. Now that you're sure of your focus, rewrite and make certain the audience knows what the main problem is in the first five minutes. If they don't, you will lose them. Often the playwright is very clear on the subject of his or her play, but fails to communicate it quickly enough, choosing subtlety over clarity. If the protagonist plans to bake the biggest bagel in Chicago (as my teacher Israel Horowitz once suggested), find this out in the opening minutes of the play. In Marsha Norman's play *'Night, Mother* we know from the beginning that Jessie wants to kill herself. She tells her mother so. The secret of the play's tension is that the audience spends the evening waiting to see whether or not she'll actually do it.

Order of Scenes:

In a linear play, one scene should push the next scene forward. In a nonlinear play, you have a constellation of scenes, which should connect thematically. Either way, there should be a forward momentum. If you do not have this momentum, you need to re-order or even eliminate a scene.

Suggestion: List the action of each scene on a separate index card. Also, give each scene a title, such as "The Humiliation Scene," "The Scene of Huge Disappointment," or "Discovery of the Secret," or "Joyful Connection." Place all these index cards on your desk or floor in the order they now appear in the play. Do they form an increasing set of conflicts that leads to a confrontation? What is the build of emotion for each character? How could you re-order the scenes to make the play more dramatic?

Endings. The Ending Is Not Satisfying:

Suggestion: Please refer to Chapter 7 on Endings. Ernest Hemingway wrote the last page of *A Farewell to Arms* forty-four times before he finally got it right.

Remember. Deal with *one problem at a time.* Do your rewrite methodically. Cross each rewriting problem off your list as you go, making certain that all your revisions are organic to the completed script.

Now, the following advice about rewriting was given to me by a group of distinguished writers, and I pass it on to you with many thanks for their input. Liz Poliner, a novelist, poet, and teacher of creative writing at George Washington University in Washington, D.C., had this to say about the process of rewriting:

> Every so often I have a student whose work is in the middle of the group when the students hand in their original drafts, but when I see the revision at the end of the semester, the work shoots ahead to among the top writers in the class, which surprises me because the work has been consistently mediocre until the revision process kicks in. But what the student has done is the truest revision in the class, meaning the most vigorous rewriting, and often, the most rigorous revisioning or re-seeing.

When I asked Ms. Poliner what she meant by "vigorous" she told me:

> By vigorous, I mean the student has engaged in the most line editing, cutting, reshaping, and, most of all, seeing the work in a new way, rather than tinkering with the work a little. And I am always thrilled for the student and thrilled for the lesson it teaches me that revision can be so important to writing. I think, too, that this experience shows how sometimes it is important to let go of our original intent in order to find the deeper, better story.

> In the case of my own work, I will tell you about my three most vigorous and interesting revision experiences. The first is a story called "Mutual Life and Casualty" that took seven years to complete and has become the title story of a my recently published novel in stories. With this story, I was dealing with complicated family dynamics that simply took me a long time to understand, and I went through draft after draft of adding and deleting and moving things around to find the narrative flow. Sometimes it felt like pushing boulders.

> Narrative flow: the direction for the story to take where the conflict gently and gradually rises, as opposed to a jerky nar-

rative line which stops and starts and prevents the emotional arc from emerging. For whatever reason, it took me years to do this revision, but it is also one of the most complex stories I've written. All family members in the story are both getting hurt and hurting each other, so it is a story without a hero or villain. Rather, it is one of the most realistic depictions I have managed to write of what can happen in a family when it is troubled.

The next example is a novel I recently completed revisions on, *Tomorrow Then*. After I had finished a draft of it that read pretty smoothly, I went to a writers' conference, and there my workshop leader pointed out something that he considered a weakness, a comment that felt very true, and which I could not deny. His comment was that the narration was written in a style such that the author clearly knew where she was going all the time. The story then became predictable because I was sending too many obvious signals. After the conference I simply sat on the criticism for three or four months, unsure what to do about it, but unable to dismiss it. Suddenly, one day, I decided I had to simply open the book up in a new way. The image in my mind was that my novel was a large china platter that I was holding in front of me. I let it fall to the ground and smash into pieces. By smashing it I was opening up spaces. Also, when I picked up the broken pieces, I put them back together in a different arrangement, and one that, in the end, better matched what the story is about.

A third interesting revision experience involved a long poem. I began writing it in Maine, and I knew I wanted to write it in six parts that loosely correlated with the six flute and piano sonatas by Bach. My first draft had some parts that worked and some parts that were just not lively. I had to completely rewrite several parts, and then reshuffle the arrangement before the poem took form. In the end, I think I got a better poem than I ever anticipated. I got to a place in the poem that I had hoped to get to, but in a form that was more exciting than I could have originally imagined. The poem is called "Thinking about the Six Bach Sonatas for Flute and Piano while Vacationing in Maine," and was published in *Hanging Loose*, a literary journal (Spring 2004).

This process reminds me that you have to walk a fine line between pushing your work where you want it to go, and letting what will happen, happen.

Barbara Greenberg, a Boston poet, short fiction writer, and co-author of the children's musical *Jeremy and the Thinking Machine*, as well as a teacher of creative writing, gave the following advice:

> To rewrite: first, to edit out whatever seems inauthentic, derivative and/or lazy. In the process of editing, to re-engage with what was valid and original in the former draft. Then, with luck, to rewrite from that source. Language and technique will often rise to the challenge.

Shirley Lauro, born in the Midwest, and now living in New York, is a playwright, novelist, and teacher, and has this to say about rewriting:

> The quote I think of about rewrites is one you may already know or be using. It is a benchmark quote that I always stick by: Writing is rewriting. I think we really write only one story all of our writing lives, over and over and over again.

Richard Walter, chair of screenwriting at UCLA, screenwriter, fiction writer, and colleague, said:

> Real writing is rewriting. A first draft is just that: It is the first of many, many, many drafts. David Koepp, a former student of mine studying screenwriting at UCLA and now the richest screenwriter of them all (he worked on *Spider-Man; Panic*

Room; Snake Eyes; The Lost World: Jurassic Park; Mission Impossible; Jurassic Park; and *Death Becomes Her,* among others) writes no fewer than seventeen drafts of each of his screenplays. He says his huge success has more to do with his ability to tolerate notes and commentary from outsiders than upon anything else. As his teacher, I like to argue that his talent and discipline ought to be factored into the equation.

The most essential aspect of rewriting has to do with a writer's attitude. She has to be willing to consider — not embrace, not necessarily adopt, but merely consider — the suggestions that others may offer. Even if 95 percent of the suggestions are nonsense, it is worth considering all of them so as to exploit — that is, make the most of — whatever small, useful components might emerge. These can add up to a lot of improvement in a script. In my own experience, I have had to stifle the urge to strangle an executive or an agent who made a suggestion that I considered lame, only to find myself integrating it weeks and even months later, after the dust has settled, and after I have had a chance truly, fully, to digest the commentary. No writer ever sat down before the computer or ruled yellow legal pad without thinking "this time it will be perfect right from the start." That is, of course, never the case. And writers have to accept that they will be rewriting even after the book is published or the play mounted or the film produced and exhibited.

On my most recent book tour I found myself performing live readings of the novel, only to be editing as I went, realizing how much more work I still had left to do on this book, losing sight of the fact that it was already published, available in the stores, and on the best seller list. The lesson? The Rolling Stones said it all: "Can't get no satisfaction!"

Elizabeth Diggs, a playwright and colleague in dramatic writing at the Tisch School of the Arts, stated:

> When I finished my first play, I thought it was perfect. Then, I got extensive notes from a wonderful actress, Margaret Barker (an original member of the Group Theatre). "My dear," she said, "the play has possibilities, but you need to do a lot of work." I was shocked and offended, especially since I had written a meaty role for her! After a few days of absorbing what she said, I reread the play and got to work. Since then, I've learned that I go through a process with every new play, and it usually involves at least two and often many more drafts. Now I am ruthless, and I love the process. I love to finish a first draft because then the real work begins. I welcome notes, I love to make changes, and I love to be ruthless — cut characters! cut scenes! cut favorite lines! I love to cook, and I like to compare drama to cooking a marvelous sauce — it has to have great ingredients, and then be reduced to its essence. I am happy to report that with that first play, I worked on it through several more drafts before it was produced at Long Wharf. Margaret Barker played the role I had written (and rewritten) for her and had standing ovations at age seventy-eight. And my play, *Close Ties* is still being performed thanks to her insight and honesty.

Susan Miller is a playwright as well as a film and television writer. She performed her own award-winning play, *My Left Breast*. Susan lives in New York. She offered these comments about rewriting:

> Just a caveat: Okay, resistance to revision is not at all a bad thing. You have to trust your impulse, your plan, your way cavort. I muck around and play loose with the idea of it all. I purposely lose my way. For me, there are two kinds of revision. The exuberant, painstaking, constant exercise I employ every day. Refreshing every sentence, honing every speech. Revitalizing

characters. And repositioning scenes so they are truly where they belong. This kind of beat-by-beat, almost tactile work is necessary to infuse the play with energy, wit, and force. Each day, to keep things fresh, I read through the whole text. If something is dull or muddy or just not up to it, I'm pretty merciless. If things seem to move along and suddenly I hit a rough spot, I stay there until getting to the finish. It's your foothold. You can't let everyone in who wants to have a say. Including your own doubt. But, then, here's what I do. I go outside the play. I stretch the framework. I try new scenes. Out of context. Out of the play's range. I say, what if? I gamble and I figure out what is breaking down or what might be holding things up. That's the most difficult place for me to dwell. It interrupts my sleep and governs my waking hours, which is how I know I have to keep going to that problem in the text until I solve it. For me, the whole point of writing a play is not knowing if I can pull it off. It is by its nature, a problem. An ever-changing thing.

Ernest Hemingway would go back over his work every day, from the beginning, and rewrite. This was critical to his process. As several chapters began to develop, he'd go back two or three chapters to continue the piece with the proper "tone." Early drafts of his writing are very undisciplined, ramble all over the place, and include many false starts.[1] Hemingway's lean, disciplined style made the writing and the living seem simple. He focused on one point and wrote very clearly about that point. But if we put all the stories together, all the pieces, a very complex picture emerges. Neither the living nor the writing was easy. "There's no rule on how it is to write," Hemingway wrote his editor Charles Poore in 1953. "Sometimes it comes easily and perfectly. Sometimes it is like drilling rock and then blasting it out with charges."[2] Because *A Farewell to Arms* was being serialized in *Scribner's Magazine*, Hemingway had six months to struggle with the ending. He left forty-four pages of alternate endings, a record even for the meticulous Hemingway, who would write out or retype a page until he was satisfied with it. Fitzgerald sent Hemingway ten handwritten pages of comments on the draft of the novel, and Hemingway's response was "Kiss my ass."[3]

August Wilson, in reference to *Jitney*, his 1970s play, which premiered in Pittsburgh in 1982 and repremiered at the Pittsburgh Public in 1996 and then opened at Boston's Huntington Theatre prior to a Broadway revival in 2000, said:

> Marion McClinton is directing and we're going to scrap everything else, the set and the costumes. We may use some of the same actors, but we're going to start over and I'm going to do some re-writes, particularly the Becker-Booster scenes. I want to rethink the whole character of Booster. I wrote that 18, 19 years ago now, and I think maybe if I reimagine it, now that I'm more mature, they'll say different things.[4]

In the spring 2001 issue of *African American Review*, Elisabeth J. Heard writes about *Jitney*:

> The revision of *Jitney* sparked an interest among critics in Wilson's revision strategies. Critic Herrington states, "The changes Wilson made to Jitney reflected a new methodology of playwriting — specifically of rewriting — which he had developed while working on *Seven Guitars* at the Goodman Theatre in Chicago in 1995." This "new methodology" involved not re-writing the play before the rehearsal. Instead, Wilson waited until the rehearsal process began and then made daily changes to the script. If he felt that a scene needed to be changed or that a monologue should be added, Wilson would go home, do the rewrite, and bring the changes to rehearsal the next day. I asked Wilson about this revision strategy.

Heard: I read that you experimented with a new revision strategy for this play. Will you continue to use this strategy with future plays?

Wilson: You are talking about writing in the moment?

Heard: Yes, getting feedback from the actors and directors, writing new parts, and bringing them the next day.

Wilson: That's a good way to work. I don't know if it is necessarily a new way to work because generally I'd do the whole rewrite, come to rehearsal, and continue to work on it. But one time when I did *Seven Guitars*, I didn't do a rewrite. I did the rewrite during the rehearsal process, and it seemed to work as well if not better than the other way. I guess I'm not consciously aware that I made a change, but I'll certainly continue doing what I'm doing, working the way I'm working, and I enjoy the rehearsal process and working through there. So I will continue that.

In the past I would rewrite the whole thing and bring it in, and, of course, there were certain revisions that were made in the rehearsal process. But the bulk of the work had been done, so I would sort of lay back off of it (if that's a way of saying it) because I already did the rewrite, and now I was just patching up various things. With *Seven Guitars* I didn't do the rewrite prior to rehearsal. I came into rehearsal knowing that the play had to be rewritten. And I did my rewrite there in rehearsal, which didn't allow me to lay back off the material and do patchwork. I had to get in there and do the actual work, which seemed to work better in the sense that I wasn't writing in a vacuum. I had the actors there, so you could press and then you could see a response, or you could do something and see an immediate response. If you're at home doing the rewrite, you can't get that response — you're sort of working in a vacuum, so to speak.

Heard: Were there other benefits from writing in the moment and getting the immediate feedback?

Wilson: I think so. It is a different kind of work, so you write different things. I think that if I'm at home sitting doing the rewrite, I'm going to write something different than if I'm there in the rehearsal room doing it. It's kind of hard to explain, but if you're tossed into the fire at any particular moment, then you are going to write something different than you will in another particular moment. And that is from day to day. Here at this moment on Tuesday at this rehearsal I'll come up with this, and I'm going to rewrite that; I'm going to rewrite it tonight. If I rewrite it next week I'm going to write something different. So you have to choose what is the right moment to do it because you sort of only get to do it once. I found more immediacy in the rehearsal process. I certainly wrote different things — I don't know if I wrote better things — and I enjoyed it.[5]

Anton Chekhov wrote, in regard to rewriting:

I shall finish my story to-morrow or the day after, but not to-day, for it has exhausted me fiendishly towards the end. Thanks to the haste with which I have worked at it, I have wasted a pound of nerves over it. The composition of it is a little complicated. I got into difficulties and often tore up what I had written, and for days at a time was dissatisfied with my work — that is why I have not finished it till now. How awful it is! I must rewrite it! It's impossible to leave it, for it is in a devil of a mess. My God! If the public likes my works as little as I do those of other people, which I am reading, what an ass I am! There is something asinine about our writing.[6]

Tina Howe, New York playwright and professor of writing for theater at Hunter College in New York had the following to say about the process of rewriting:

> Writing a play is an exercise in stamina, blind faith and insanity. More than anything it calls for compression. Getting down on your hands and knees and beating things down to their essence. It's loud and messy work. You scream, weep and tear out your hair in fistfuls. After years of doing this, I've finally come up with an image that encapsulates the whole gruesome process.
>
> An idea for a new play is like an enormous lake — something really huge like Lake Erie, but instead of being filled with water, it's filled with rubber cement — shimmering, viscous and smelly. As your ideas start to sharpen, the lake miraculously starts to shrink. From a lake to a swimming hole and finally to a pond that you can circumnavigate in an afternoon. As your characters become more vivid, you find yourself kicking the outer edges of this pond until you can actually lean over and scoop it up in your arms. Handle it! Lick and poke it! Place it over your heart! When that happens it means the play is going to work! You're going to write it! And it's going to be your best ever!
>
> Then the real compression begins. Slapping and kneading the gooey mess until you can hold it in one hand. As the play takes shape, the script goes from the size of one of those huge plastic balls physical therapists use, to a medicine ball — to a basketball — to a volley ball — to a croquet ball — to a softball — to a baseball — to a ping pong ball — to a golf ball — to a marble and finally to a BB. As it compresses it gets harder, of course. When it reaches the golf ball stage it's as dense and heavy as a chunk of uranium. It you threw it out the window into the street, it would level an entire neighborhood.

When, after two years of this relentless compression, it's finally the size of a BB, you have to proceed with caution as you roll it between your thumb and forefinger. It *is* rubber cement after all and it could just disappear into thin air. It's happened to me. I've polished and refined plays into grains of sand [that] simply blew away. It's at this stage that you have to crawl out of your study, place it in a tiny box and give it to someone else to read.

The entire process reverses itself once the play is accepted by a theater. You hand the company your gleaming BB, copies are made until all the actors have one and then the ritual of release begins. As they knead their BBs, they get softer and softer. And bigger and bigger. Soon the floor is shimmering with rubber cement. It shudders and pools. As they bring the play to life, tides start to rise and suddenly we're back to our original lake. It's no longer my play! It belongs to all of us, and it's as vast and beautiful as any ocean you've ever seen.

For me, the process of rewriting *After Marseilles* took five years, although not contiguously, including six rewrites, and still counting. Since you have some background already on that play, the following are the notes I made and the questions I asked before starting each rewrite:

Rewrite I

- How does the first monologue on "Blue" feed into the focus of the play?
- Read book titled *Blue* and visit museum looking at paintings that utilize primarily the color blue, from the Renaissance through contemporary work. What may be the significance?
- Make certain all the wants of the characters are real so their disappointments are real.

- Is this a play about a yearning for an old America, and about the beliefs that we can always reinvent ourselves and transform?
- Madame Zaza's entrance should be much earlier.
- What does Madame Zaza want? Is she telling the truth?
- The last two scenes are right. How do I get there? It's where I want to go but the destination isn't yet earned.
- Do not lose the absurd for the mundane.
- What is Madame Zaza's reason for intervention?
- Why do people allow themselves to be bullied and not stand up? Are they afraid to trust their own feelings?

Rewrite II

- Make sure the constant changing of the colored flags is dangerous enough.
- What are their honest emotions? Don't cerebrate.
- Chip is not developed enough as a mythic figure.
- Longing for community. Feel it!
- Is there a scene where they are all freed of authority and act like children?
- Are they destined to repeat their mistakes, or is that a red herring and not what the play is about at all?
- What is the major action of the play? If it is to get out of Marseilles, I don't believe it — but somewhere, the focus of the play is tied to that but I don't know how yet.
- Make it clear that Zoey is a journalist. Establish others identities — Madame Zaza as fashion designer, Chip as artist, Dakota as fisherwoman from Alaska, Sam as jazz musician.
- We have to believe that Zoe and Chip are in love.
- What is it that could break Zaza's spirit?

- Break down action of every scene in the play.
- What are the rising action and the climax? The climax has to do with something Madame Zaza does.

Rewrite III

- They all must be desperate and at each other's throats.
- What does Zaza want? To hold on to her life spirit? To never give up? To be in control? Then what could make her lose control? Remember that Zaza hates uncertainty.
- They must be terrified of being punished if they don't follow the government's rules. The danger has to be very real.
- The desire to rebuild physically is the right instinct.
- I know the end is destruction — but how? And what comes out of it?
- What does Sam really see on the other side of the bridge?
- Zaza has a secret. I don't know what it is yet. She's keeping it from even me, the author. I'll find out.
- At the end of the play do Zoe and Chip find their luggage and leave it on the stage? It's useless. The very thing they had sought is useless, without meaning.
- At least Zaza has the courage of her own life in an age without morality or reason. Zaza is the key to this play.
- Is someone saved by an act of grace like some character in a Flannery O'Connor story?
- Stakes is what the character has to win or lose — remember!
- Conflict is what prevents the character from getting what they want.

Rewrite IV

- Zaza has been lying about the government in Paris. There is no government. She did it to keep order and prevent chaos.
- How is she discovered? What is the moment? Who discovers it? Why did she do it?
- When does everyone find out? They must be furious at being betrayed.
- I keep hearing Madame Zaza saying she is trying to hold back the ocean, hold back the tides — isn't this trying to prevent time from moving on? Maybe she is trying to stave off her own death, like *Appointment in Samara*. In the end she gives up. Why? Her spirit breaks down. Why? Could it be because she has been found out? Do the others forgive her? Forgiveness is gained if someone explains himself or herself. Perhaps if she apologizes and we believe her — that by keeping them all there, she can prevent her own death. You have to die by yourself, alone. Maybe Zaza figures as long as she can keep everyone in Marseilles, even for false reasons, she can hold off her own aging and death.
- Part of living is the ability finally to let go.
- Picture of Zaza alone on stage at the end.

Rewrite V

- Go through entire script and edit mercilessly. Get rid of at least twenty pages.
- Ultimately the people that inhabit this earth are going to have to figure out a way to forge a workable agreement on how to treat one another.
- Remember that each character is out to save his or her own skin.

- When they find out Zaza has been lying, not enough happens.
- Sam must be furious with himself for believing Zaza and going along with her. But the others must blame Sam by association. Sam also has to be angry with Zaza for making him her stooge. He should confront her.
- Each person has been betraying someone else in the story. How?
- Look at places where the characters are ruminative or meditative. Do they slow down the play? No lyrical outbursts, please!
- Make danger real if all do not obey, in the first scenes.
- We must care about Sam and know what he wants.
- Compassion for Zaza at the end of the play.
- We hear the animals coming over the bridge from Africa, at the end, and it signals a huge natural disaster that is the end of the play. Animals have the capacity to hear what humans can't. Knowing disaster is coming and the animals are running away from it, they all want Zaza to come away with them, through the Alps and Spain. Zaza refuses and asks them to leave her in peace alone.
- Last image is Zaza with her back to us, hammering away at the new dress shop she is building. We know it is useless, but she keeps on.

Rewrite VI

- We are free to behave the way we want, but we are responsible for our actions.
- What distinguishes us as humans is our empathy. Evil is the absence of compassion.
- They must discover how to behave when the shibboleth of the government is revealed and there are no rules.
- In the blues the human spirit is soaring. Go back to the original impetus of the play — the color blue.

- Zaza stops death in its tracks. The real search is for meaning. See Victor Frankl's book *Man's Search for Meaning*.
- Zaza knows in the end (realizes) that she is doomed to mortality. She had her turn.
- In a sense it is a dream play. Set in at beginning with lighting.
- One act of love redeems. All the others forgive Zaza and want her to escape with them, and that knowledge allows her to let go of them — the knowledge that she is wanted/loved.

The first draft of the play began with just a monologue about "Blue" and I cannot tell you why. I do know I constructed the world of the play (one following a series of large natural and man-made disasters) because of the escalating violence prevalent in the latter part of the twentieth century. The opening image of lost luggage in the play was based on a real incident, when I did once actually lose some luggage in Marseilles; and that feeling of Marseilles being both the end of the world and the actual crossroads of the world stayed with me. It is also of interest to note that in the last days of 2004, computerization broke down when thousands were flying at Christmastime, and there were newspaper photos of acres of pieces of lost and abandoned luggage at airports. Was the play prescient? I don't think so. Rather, there are ideas floating in the air, at certain times in history, and disasters, like canned food on shelves, waiting to happen.

In the process of writing the play, and through several workshops, its focus changed vastly. The process of rewriting this play was a prime example of writing to find out what it is you are writing about. I had to go through four drafts before the discovery that Zaza was trying to hold off her own mortality. When that moment came, the character herself whispered it to me and it was a shocking revelation. I remember thinking, "So this is what this whole play was about after all." It was thrilling. Once that discovery was made, it was easier to put the entire play into focus.

For the technical process of rewriting, I find it valuable to save hard copies of all drafts, in addition to hard drive and disc copies of several drafts. These recorded drafts represent the history of each play, as well as remind you about the process of rewriting. The professional writer knows that the first draft, after all, represents only the *beginning*.

This lecture was first given at New York University's Tisch School of the Arts in May 1987, and then again, rewritten and delivered in February 2005. It has been slightly revised for inclusion in this book.

Three Exercises in Rewriting

1. Take a current play you are working on, after you have completed one draft and are about to start the next draft. Make your own list of what problems need to be dealt with in the next draft. Decide how you will accomplish the changes you desire. Then methodically go through the script crossing off each change as you effect it.

2. Take a play you have put away because it was not working. Make certain at least six months have elapsed since you put down the play. Read it with fresh eyes. What could you do in a rewrite that might improve the play, providing you still feel passionate about this play?

3. Take a play where you are not sure about which character is the protagonist. Outline your play first using Character A as the protagonist, and then using Character B as the protagonist. The character with the strongest desires is more likely to go to the edge to get what he or she wants. Which character has the possibility of the more dramatic journey?

9

JOURNALS

Ah — journals. I am looking at my bookshelves and I count thirty-three personal journals. The newest one is a blue, hand-made, unlined, Watermark book. It says it was crafted in Port Townsend, Washington, and was given to me as a recent birthday gift. Underneath it on the shelf is a lovely lined brown leather volume with shoelace-like ties and a satin page marker. It's called "the brown traveler" and was given to me by a student. I just opened it for the first time since I received it as a gift a year ago and found inside (this is true!) a folded fifty-dollar bill. Now, I don't believe this struggling student left a fifty-dollar bill inside the book before me, nor do I ever remember putting such a thing in this book since I don't carry large amounts of money. I can only conclude that this untouched journal is a gift meant to be written in, and I should take it with me on my travels and use it for my next play.

With this discovery, I am foraging through my office, check-ing every journal I have stored on its shelves. There's the one with "The Bridge at Argenteuil" by Monet, of handmade Italian paper, feathered, bought in the market in Florence. It begins:

October 13, 1993. Today I left for Jakarta. I read Donald Hall's book *Life Works* — about the value of work when we love it and how close it is to prayer … the overnight in Tokyo was pleasanter than I anticipated, and the Holiday Inn even luxurious. I kept CNN on all night for company. I ordered room service — scrambled eggs and tea … now I'm on the flight to Jakarta via Kuala Lumpur. The embassy envoy, Bob Schmidt, will meet me at the airport. I read the phrasebook … "Sampai jumpa lagi," means "see you later."

The next entry is a month later — "Today I am returning …" When I read this I remember there was no time to write in the journal while in Jakarta. The students and the language and the heat are too demanding. So, the rest of the entries in the journal are all made on the way home.

So what to make of it all? It all seems like a dream. Some of it, even like a bad dream. What did I expect? Hard work in an exotic city? What did I get? Intolerable heat, close to 105 degrees — teaching for six hours — and in a city which is surely the most polluted I have ever encountered and without architecture. In the mass of traffic [people wander with handkerchiefs against their faces as protection from the pollution], the sky is unseeeable. If Jakarta looked like it was an archipelago surrounded by water, there is no sight on maps of the Indian Ocean. When I say I want to go to see it, I am warned there is nothing to see. It is filthy and strewn with garbage. When a student took me to see the ocean one day, it was, alas, true. Everyone tells me, instead "wait until you see Bali," but, of course, I never get there. My teaching duties didn't permit. In despair over the heat, I succumbed to teaching with washcloths soaked in cold water on top of my head.

Then things began slowly to improve. Little doors began to open. The long, seemingly unpronounceable names of the student writers became easier as the participants became real people. Many of them were young professionals and graduating students, chosen by their government to attend the writing seminars. On the last day I could tell you all their names, and without looking at a class roster — Ifu and Adi and Agus, and Amantano, and Garin, and Nan, and Danny, and Widi and Pandu and Gotok and Santiago. I also knew their strengths and weaknesses as writers.

Because Indonesia imported so many U.S. daytime dramas (soaps) and programs like *Dallas*, their characterizations tended towards the stereotypical, so the thrust of my work was character oriented. These writers have wonderful stories to tell, a richness of background steeped heavily in myth. These writers have talent and passion and ideals. They were, in the end, the largest gift of Jakarta.

The journal entries from Jakarta, written over ten years ago, tell more than you want to know about Jakarta, but it brings it all back to me, I can remember the students and the heat. The last entry reads: "Perhaps I made a difference in the lives of these young writers and their spirit ... the United airplane leaves Noritz airport in Tokyo and heads homeward to the U.S. and New York, and everyone I love — my home."

Next, I find a "Gunning Data," notebook from a student in Jakarta, inscribed; "I bought this notebook in a small store in Jakarta. It is the only one left," he tells me. He also tells me, "This notebook reminds me of when I was a schoolboy. I hope you like this unique notebook as you like to create unique characters. I hope it reminds you about Jakarta. Best regards, Kendal. Jakarta October, 1993."

Yes it does. I remember you, Kendal. I wonder whatever happened to you.

Another journal has, among its entries, a dream, 1990. "I want to tell my mother things that have happened, that Carolyn has moved to Los Angeles, but I can't tell her, because she is dead."

Then, there is the blue flowered fabric notebook, with only a pressed flower, the telephone number of someone named "Sumati" inside it, and one notation: "When no one is looking, I am happy." There is another college ruled notebook with ideas in it for future plays ... it is from 1973–75 — my graduate years at Brandeis. There are entries like: "I sit and watch the boy and girl on the beach," and I see that this entry eventually became a scene in my play *The Bridge at Belharbour*, and noted conversations, either real or construed, and the entry, "I wonder where dreams come from — places I've never seen, but I must have been there before, or how would I know them?"

There is a notation about a new play ... *The Good Man*, about a man who appears good to the outside community, but to his immediate family is a horror. "I recognize the person this is based on." Then, there is an entry about a picnic with friends: "I was thirsty and someone delivered a case of champagne to the door. I hardly knew I was thirsty until it arrived."

Each journal entry brings my life back to me. It is all on the pages — and a clipping inside. "There are, according to psychiatrists, more than 170 different emotions that can move you to tears. Not all weeping is caused by sorrow. We weep for joy, pride, in gratitude, in triumph, and in ecstasy."

In another, from 1991, on January 22:

> First day of spring semester, The Gulf War rages. The war with the Playwrights Collective in the department seems solved. They will begin "A Writer's Theatre."

Then I remember that collective and how many of those students have gone onto work in the theatre ...

There are more journals, too many to note and read through. I pick up one last favorite, given by a writer colleague, "A Writer's

Notebook," with insights from writers and spaces for personal quotes and a lovely salmon-colored, swirled cover. The pages are unlined and there is a drawing and a quotation on every page. I see the journal was given to me in 1989. The first entry reads: "You can't wait for inspiration. You have to go after it with a club." A later one reads, "Last week we lost everything. My husband lost his glasses and I lost my wedding band, and many people were nasty ... and then out of the notebook fell — yes, it is true — a gold hoop earring I lost long ago — and now I wonder if I held on to its mate. You see the treasures in journals, our past and future, fifty-dollar bills and long ago lost earrings, and recaptured life.

Exercise in Journaling

Keep a separate journal for your next three plays. Start keeping the journal when you have your first idea. Continue writing in this journal as you explore and create the play. Write down the moments that are the most surprising, that give you the most trouble, and that give you the most joy. Keep a record of how you solve the problems. In the same journal, log all readings, workshops, and full productions. You will then have a record of development, and it may even make an article or book someday!

10

The Making of a Play: "A Small Delegation" from Beijing to Home

Beijing Journals, June 1987 and April 1995: The Odyssey of a Play

In our journals we often discover our plays. The following set of journal entries trace the odyssey of the play, *A Small Delegation*, from its genesis while teaching in China, to its eventual production in China by the China Youth Arts Theatre. The first journals were kept in the summer of 1987 on an initial trip. At the start of the journals I had no intention of writing a play, but only wanted to record the events of the journey. The second set of journals is dated April 1995, and was kept during the Chinese production of the play, four years after the writing of the play and several U.S. productions. The circularity of the journals starting in Beijing and eventually coming back to Beijing is a reminder of the connectedness of our lives and our work, each flowing into the other, *if* we are open to opportunity. If the world invites, answer "yes."

It was the summer of 1987, two years before the Tiananmen Square uprising, and I was invited to China to teach with a small group of American writers and scholars. They included Richard Walter, a screenwriter and chair of screenwriting at UCLA, Brian Henderson, film scholar and cinema studies professor at SUNY Buffalo, and Anne Kaplan, film scholar and cinema studies professor at SUNY Stonybrook. Our students were young film professionals, many of whom subsequently became members of the "fifth generation" of Chinese filmmakers, including Chen Kaege, Wu Tian Min, head of the Xi'an Film Studio, and Zhang Yimou. During that summer I became good friends with my Chinese translator; however, toward the end of our stay, a curious incident occurred that was the genesis for my play *A Small Delegation*.

In my desire to help my new friend, I gave her a gift that was politically incorrect, unbeknownst to me, thereby endangering her job as a university teacher and translator. In developing the play, I posed the following question: *What if* a well-intentioned American goes to China meaning to do good and, in so doing, causes tragedy?

From the original incident, described in the journals that follow, I fashioned the play, *A Small Delegation*. The play tells the story of a small group of Americans who go to Beijing the summer before Tiananmen Square, the developing friendship between an American professor and her Chinese translator, and the limits and possibilities of East/West exchange. There are five Chinese and three Caucasian characters in the script. I moved the date of the play from the summer of 1987 to that of 1988, the summer directly preceding Tiananman Square, to increase the dramatic impact. The characters, like those in most plays, are an amalgamation, based on the true characters I met, and the story, like all dramatic stories, comes of asking "What if?" based on the real generating incident.

A Small Delegation premiered at the Annenberg Center Philadelphia Festival Theatre for New Plays in 1992. Susan H. Schulman directed, Ming Cho Lee designed the sets, Shi-Zheng Chen was the choreographer, and Tan Dun composed the original music. The cast included some of the most outstanding Asian actors in American theater,[1] and also featured actress Bai Ling in her U.S. stage premiere, prior to her Hollywood career. This production was followed by a West Coast production at TheatreWorks in Palo Alto, California. Reviewers noted the unity of the Western perspective, "which seems like an inside job," and that even as we blame the Chinese system for the translator's fate, "we also blame the American, and ourselves by extension since her instincts are our own — for being something of a meddler."[2]

Despite excellent reviews, it was not easy to get the play produced in the United States. Each play always has its own hurdles, and *A Small Delegation* was no exception. First, the political correctness of the play was questioned. How could an American write truthfully about China? But one doesn't have to be born in China to understand oppression. Then, even if the observations were faithful to the Chinese culture, how appropriate was it to have a Caucasian writer? In addition, where were most theaters to get Asian actors? Certainly not in the Midwest. Then, on the West Coast, where there were larger Asian populations. One Asian theater company, for example, only produced plays by Asians.

Finally, in 1994, news came that the China Youth Arts Theatre in Beijing, under the artistic direction of Shi Wei Jin, an old friend of Shi-Zheng, had asked for permission to produce *A Small Delegation* in Beijing, with Shi-Zheng Chen as translator and director. Shi-Zheng had grown up in China, was there during the Cultural Revolution, could speak both English and Chinese, and therefore could bridge the play's built-in culture gap. Shi-Zheng had also been a member of the Beijing Opera before emigrating to the United States.

During that year, preceding the planned Chinese production in 1995, I worked on a rewrite of the play so it would be acceptable to the Ministry of Culture in China, without compromising its essence. It was then translated by Shi-Zheng Chen, and subsequently approved by the Ministry of Culture in Beijing — or so I thought.

There are two sets of Beijing journals — those from 1987 from my first trip to China, which include the generating incident for the play, and those from April 1995, eight years later, when I went there to oversee the production of *A Small Delegation.* The two sets of journals serve as bookends for the script. It's of interest how the original experience was transformed into a dramatic structure with escalating conflicts. The final version of *A Small Delegation* represents fifteen drafts.

A Small Delegation received a Rockefeller Foundation grant to Bellagio, an A. W. Alton Foundation Production grant, and a grant for the Beijing production from the Asia Society, the Asian Cultural Council, the Kunstadter Foundation, and the Starr Foundation. The play has been published in a collection, *Plays by Janet Neipris.*[3] Excerpts from my journals follow.:

Beijing Journals: Summer 1987

June 8, 1987
We arrive in Beijing, at the invitation of the China Film Society, and our assignment is to teach screenwriting to a group of young professional Chinese filmmakers. What a relief it was to be met at the airport by Chi Soong, a journalist with *The World of Cinema* and our translator, who will accompany us on most of the trip. We almost don't get through customs with our videocassettes that include dozens of American films brought on request. Because of the Cultural Revolution, it is explained to us, the Chinese population had missed out on twenty years of films. We have to convince the customs officials, armed with machine guns, that *Annie Hall*

and *Deer Hunter* are neither obscene nor in opposition to the present government.

The drive through the darkened, deserted streets at 1:00 a.m. Beijing time, shows the city to be both majestic — wide tree-lined streets lit by massive gas lamps — also mysterious, with the rows of white lights casting shadows across an awesome Tiananmen Square, dominated by a large portrait of a smiling Mao. It is clear we are far from home.

The room at the Jin Jiang Hotel proved slightly disappointing, but after a few days I have grown rather fond of it — the large cut velvet chairs with draped crocheted doilies, the ever-present carafe of hot water (What are we supposed to DO with all this hot water?), and the shower which is part of the bathroom floor, flooding it every time we use it. We call it lovingly "the rice paddy." It all slowly becomes our home.

The laundry in the hotel is most extraordinary, in by 9, out by 5, and the results are white as snow. We are sending EVERYTHING! We should have BROUGHT laundry from America. They sew small cloth labels into everything, with your name on it, like at summer camp.

My room looks out on the main thoroughfare, Fuxingmen Avenue, which is wide and filled with throngs of bicycle riders. They carry everything on bikes here, from fresh bread to cows and pigs, to Grandma. It is like nothing I have ever seen before.

June 12, 1987

The lectures here go well, but have been arduous. So far I have given the one on *The Development of Character* and the other on *Fifty Rules for Writing a Screenplay*. The ride begins at 7:40 when our driver picks us up at the hotel to make the trip to a mountainside retreat, The Temple of the Sleeping Buddha, half an hour away, where the students wait. The first morning it is like a New York City taxi ride, almost bumping into farmers, soldiers, oxen, women with babies, donkeys, etc., with the driver beeping his horn the entire way. Brian Henderson, a professor of Film Theory at SUNY Buffalo (and the author of a most extraordinary book recently published on Preston Sturges), and I both study our lectures, rather than look. Occasionally, I sneak a peek at a passing pagoda. The driver has now been admonished and is going a little slower.

Our classes in the states could learn from these appreciative students. Perhaps this is how it should be. When you enter, they are all seated, waiting expectantly, and rise to greet the professor and applaud. At the end of each FOUR-HOUR lecture, they also stand and applaud. No one comes late. No one leaves early. During the lecture the students take voluminous notes. It is terribly hot, close to one hundred degrees. They have warm orange pop, a Chinese staple, and steaming tea at your side, and I am consuming gallons of both.

The students are both sweet and awesome. This is a new combination. These are already award-winning screenwriters and directors. Some have received the coveted Red Rooster award, similar to our Academy Award. We learn that the rooster is a revered creature here, first on the lineup of sacred animals on the rooftops of all the ancient temples — perhaps deservedly so. The rooster is indeed the first up, same as us teachers!

The students are serious, but laugh at the jokes if you explain they are meant to be funny. They particularly like the Fifty Questions lecture because it is so specific. They keep asking, "What number are we on?" The lecture today runs almost five hours. What a workout! The rest of our "small delegation" agree. They include myself, Bryan Henderson, Anne Kaplan, and Richard Walter. On opposite mornings, classes are taught by Richard Walters, head of screenwriting at UCLA, and Anne Kaplan, a film theorist from Rutgers, soon to transfer to SUNY Stonybrook. Anne and I are the only ones to bring spouses. Anne has brought her husband,

Martin, chair of NYU's psychology department, and I am accompanied by my husband, Donald, an engineer.

June 15, 1987

Today we visit the magnificent Temple of Heaven, a masterpiece of fifteenth-century architecture. The cobalt blue roofs of the temples look like pleated lampshades, and in the 100° plus afternoon sun, glistens indeed like heaven. It is still an active Buddhist temple and we try not to disturb the monks as we weave our way through the treasures inside. They look impervious to us. I wonder how really peaceful they are in the face of China's burgeoning tourism.

June 19, 1987

Today we climb the Great Wall, all fifteen hundred steps. We are considered heroes. My good friend and translator, Sun, comes with us. We are a large group and it is like a family outing, our small procession of cars winding its way up the mountainside to the Wall. Chen Jihua, head of the China Film Association, is there, as are Comrade Wong, giving directions right and left, and his assistant, Ping. We speculate that these two are involved. There are also rumors that Comrade Wong was a high official during the "CR," as they call the Cultural Revolution. Now he is Head of International Liaison, and does not speak fluent English, but we find out he does speak Spanish. Richie Walter converses with him in Spanish and then translates. In the future, when the students at New York University argue with my insistence on a language requirement, I will tell them why! I feel more strongly than ever about training literate screenwriters and playwrights.

The climb to the top of the Great Wall is exhilarating, and once there we can look over the countryside for miles and see the wall clinging to the contours of the mountaintops as far as we can see. At the top, we meet a grandfather, eighty-nine years old, with cane, and wife eighty-seven years young, who have made it to the summit. We congratulate them on their triumph. In China it is the ultimate climb. Where is ours in the United States? The Grand Canyon? The Empire State Building? The steps of the U.S. Capitol? On the climb, we stop to rest often. Sun and I are arm in arm. We have some warm orange pop and I buy a t-shirt that says "i climb the great wall."

On one stop I note that some of our colleagues are way ahead of us, and I suggest we should hurry. Sun, however, points out that the wall is circular. "Look ahead of us at the younger ones," she says, and "Look behind us, where the older ones are climbing. There will always be people ahead of us and behind us, so let us find our own pace." She's saying that we will all get to the same place eventually. Is this what I am trying to tell the young writers about finding their own voice and following it? Following it is easy. Finding it is the real challenge!

After the climb we are fêted at a sumptuous and seemingly endless banquet, one of many. We drink numerous toasts and are dizzied by the swirling lazy Susan, filled with mysterious delicacies. Later, we find out we have dined on duck's tongue and bear's paw. Well, the Peking duck was certainly outstanding!

June 20, 1987

I arrive at the Temple of the Sleeping Buddha, ready to review the day's lecture with my translator, Sun. She quickly rushes me to the women's lavatories, practically pushing me into the sink. She looks ashen. Something is up. Sun advises me, in a whisper, never to speak with her in private again, and never to show any demonstrative affection towards her. Our friendship is over. She also rescinds an invitation she has given my husband and I to come to her apartment for dinner on the next Sunday evening.

When I ask her what has happened, she tells me that the Director of the China Film Society is very angry that the two of us are becoming fast friends. The Director told Sun she saw the two of us arm and arm on the Great Wall. She also witnessed Sun carrying a valuable book I had given her as a gift, one on contemporary American women playwrights. Sun was then admonished that her friendship with "this American" was taking energy away from Sun's translations and depriving attention to the entire American delegation. So, in order to ensure that Sun was occupied for the rest of our stay, the Director gave her twenty American videos that we had brought. Sun is ordered to have these videos translated from English to Chinese by the time the Americans leave, in a few weeks. Her exact words were "This should keep you busy for the rest of the time the Americans are here, and way beyond."

One could make a big political issue out of this. I'm thinking I should have given an equal gift to the Director. I do, in fact, now go through my luggage frantically, pulling out a new scarf and wrapping it and giving it to her. But it is too late, and a scarf is not a book for the culture-deprived intellectuals who suffered through the Cultural Revolution, whose books were all destroyed. I think it is simply a question of personal jealousy, although politically, one perhaps should have given a bigger gift to the Director than to the translator. I don't know.

June 23, 1987

At a banquet held in our honor at the Beijing Film Academy, President Chen, an old friend from a previous visit to NYU, is a welcome sight. The film they show us, produced at the Beijing Film Academy, *Tchen Tchen's Beauty Parlor*, is the first Western-looking film I have seen here in China, and one of their first attempts, we are told, to produce a comedy. It is about the competition between two beauty salons and the clarinet soundtrack is outstanding. President Chen promises a cassette of the music, which he later delivers at the airport when we leave for Xi'an. At the farewell banquet, before our group leaves to teach at Xi'an,

I propose we serenade them with an "old American folk song," "Slow Boat to China." Later, on our return to Beijing, and at a subsequent banquet on the Fourth of July, we sing "Yankee Doodle Dandy." Our "small delegation," as we come to be known, are all off key, but certainly in earnest, and we sound, to me, like some heavenly choir. Our offering is accepted with a hug from Xia Yan, a distinguished Chinese filmmaker, now close to ninety. He is the revered guest at the banquet and considered the D. W. Griffith of China. My translator is at the banquet, but I never look at her the entire time. I pay no attention to her, nor she to me.

June 28, 1987

A most miraculous meeting on Tuesday, June 28 with the Chinese playwright Bai Fengxi. We were both interviewed in the book *Contemporary Woman Playwrights*, published by Simon & Schuster,[4] and so knew of each other from the shared anthology of interviews. The special meeting between us is arranged through the consulate. She is to arrive at 10:00 a.m. with her own translator. She arrives on time, and the front desk calls to say she is here, but will wait in the lobby for her interpreter, who has not yet come. A half hour passes. The table in my room is set with tea and cakes. I decide to go downstairs, even though she has insisted there is no sense in meeting yet, as we will be unable to talk with each other. In the lobby I look for a distraught woman. I spot Bai immediately. "Janet!" she calls. "Bai?" We embrace in relief. The two of us start to jabber, pointing at our watches, she shaking her head. It appears she does not expect our translator to appear. At this point we are making quite a scene in the hotel lobby, like two parrots, running around crying, "What shall we do?" in two separate languages. Suddenly, an angel appears, a Mr. Wu Chun Ha. He explains, in both languages, that he is indeed an engineer and technical translator, has 45 minutes free, has heard our dilemma while sitting in the lobby, and is willing to help. We run like two schoolgirls, with Wu, our newly found engineer-translator follow-ing, up to my room, where the words begin to tumble out. We now can share our stories as playwrights.

Bai tells me that she had a most successful play just close in Beijing, which will be presented in an honored festival in September. It appears "honor" is a constant desirable here in China. Bai estab-lishes me that she writes about the differences between genera-tions. We talk about our love for the theater and our frustrations, and the difficulties, as a woman writer, in trying to juggle it all. We agree that theater is supposed to be the most difficult medium to write for because of the constraints, but we agree those same con-straints are what attract us to theater, what make it so electrifying and dangerous. Bai also started writing in 1976, like me, after rais-ing her family, so we have that in common. We agree we will, like the American cowboys, go down with our boots on! We exchange gifts: a scarf from me to her, a cloisonné key ring from her to me. Now I need to give our engineer and translator a gift, so I look about the room. I know it cannot be something inappropriately valuable, so I spy a copy of Molière's biography I've brought from home. I grab it and inscribe it to Wu, hand it to him, and he an-nounces this to be one of the most extraordinary mornings of his life and certainly the most interesting — to meet with these two writers. Again, he pronounces he is honored to be here. The three of us will not forget this forty-five minute meeting. Later I hear that Bai has invited Mr. Wu, the engineer, to one of her plays!

On parting, I tell Bai perhaps this was a much better meeting for us writers than the ordinary one we had planned. It will make a much better story someday!

June 30, 1987

This morning, my lecture is on *Women in American Film*. I have chosen films by two women I know: Joyce Chopra's *Smooth Talk*, and Suzanne Bauman's documentary, *Women of Summer*. We leave the hotel, promptly as usual, at 7:40 a.m. It is, as always, a hair-raising ride. We almost knock down farmers and their carts filled with vegetables, as well as sheep, horses, and pigs on the road. Brian Henderson, poor man, is sitting in front. We pass temples ringed in mist, and as we get further into the countryside, workers picking the crops, getting ready for the market, bushels of tomatoes and cabbage, and watermelon. Our days here in China are rolling along ... the lectures in the morning, sightseeing in the afternoon, long walks through the neighboring park at night with Henderson and Richard Walter, sharing past and present tales. Richard says they are treating us so well he is beginning to feel like a rock star. I tell him he is beginning to look like a rock star. Henderson is brilliant and has an encyclopedic memory. He knows every film ever made, who directed, who scripted, who acted. Richard says we should forgo looking up these facts in the library. Once back home, we will simply call Brian. I have invited Brian to give a lecture at NYU on Romantic Comedy in the spring. Richard will visit in the fall and give a guest lecture as well. We are already planning a reunion to compare photos.

The lecture on American Women Filmmakers goes well, and the directors admire the filmmaker's work. "Tell her beautiful," they say. They weep at the end of the American documentary, as we always do, and do again. Everyone has dreams, everyone gets old. We share the same longings and fears. I forget that we are so far away, that we are in China. We are among friends now. Sun translates and I treat her coldly and professionally. Not a drop of friendship is clearly left. Perhaps it was my fault for being so personal and open. Yes, I think it was my fault.

July 2, 1987

Much is packed into today's lecture, which will be the last. During the lecture on romantic comedy, my husband Donald becomes ill with some malaria-like bug, but is cured easily by a Chinese doctor holding his hand and taking his pulse, seemingly forever. We have lunch at I. M. Pei's exquisitely designed Fragrant Gardens Hotel, then one more extraordinary banquet, and after that a three-hour panel discussion. ALL OF US: screenwriters, film theorists, spouses, translators at a long table facing the students. The heat is the worst yet, and the dear students bring each of us a fan to help, and more of that warmorange pop, which, by now, tastes quite refreshing. We have a lively exchange of ideas on everything from film noir to absurdist comedy. We speak about the many films we have seen — a dozen in all at the different film studios. We admire the risks that many of the new filmmakers are taking in dealing with those years during and after the Cultural Revolution. Many of the films are about struggle. There is a lyricism and a determination in the best of the Chinese films, for example, *Tinjen Mountain*. After the discussion, there is, of course, a banquet: professors, students, film people, all in one hall adjoining the Sleeping Buddha. First we eat, then, we dance and give toasts and gifts. The China Film Society gives Don the loveliest blue vase and me a tablecloth and a red lacquered box. Such an atmosphere, like a wedding. No one wants to leave. We tumble our way home in the darkness, the students trailing, and waving goodbye, with sad faces. Sun is amongst them waving. She looks appropriately sad. I think she must be devastated — that a door opened and then was closed.

So now, this part is over. We promise to return, to visit them in their film studios in the provinces. I don't know what life will bring. Perhaps. But I somehow have this feeling that the story isn't over yet. Now off to Xi'an.

July 6, 1987

Xi'an The Xi'an Hotel has a bathtub! On Sunday we go to the countryside to see the terra cotta figures and a six thousand year old village. Xi'an is more rural, more people in the streets. There is a vibrant outdoor life here. It reminds us somehow of Paris. There is no poverty. Everyone has a home, often simple, but dignified. In the evening, because of the heat, the entire city is outside. Cooks make supper over woks in the street and there are piles of watermelons for dessert. What a feeling of community in Xi'an. There are many tourists here, however, and it is difficult to get near the terra cotta statues. Our visit to the Xi'an Film Studio is exciting. These are the mavericks! One of the directors, Yan Xue Shu, will visit NYU in the fall and we'll meet again. We admire the spirited and gutsy work here!

At the evening banquet, after our day in Xi'an, the head of the studio, Wu Tian-Ming, dressed in jeans and cowboy boots, tells us to sit where we like, eat what we want, no toasts — just relax. This relaxing of formalities is representative of the spirit of this village studio, in contrast to the more formal Beijing film studios. Xi'an is an island in Chinese films. Here they are daring, not didactic. These writers and directors try to tell the story of the people — not their stories. Mr. Wu tells me if you start with a simple idea, you get a more complex film. If you try for complex, you'll end up with simple. "You can't hit a target by aiming at it, he tells me."

July 9, 1987

This is the last leg of our trip. I am now in Shanghai, writing this journal in the airport, waiting for our departing plane to Beijing. This is the very same airport we passed through in the middle of the night at the beginning of our journey, when the customs officials held us up for hours because of the American videos we were bringing in. I think of Sun translating the videos and wonder how far she has gotten. I start to think I could have even cost her her job, by my foolish generosity. After all, we were the have it all Americans and they were the Cultural Revolution deprived Chinese, and so I charged forward like I was the American Red Cross. Pretty arrogant.

In Shanghai the hotel has all of the comforts of home and we are greeted by an air-conditioned van, which I quickly name "The Vanarama." On our arrival we are whisked off to see the astonishing Shanghai acrobats, sharing the front rows with a visiting delegation from Moscow. We are all closer to the tigers jumping through their hoops than we care to be. Our visit to the Shanghai studio is gracious and filled with yet more films. Since Don and I will be returning to the States earlier than the rest, we bow out and take a quick tour of Shanghai in the rain. It is probably the way Shanghai ought to be seen. Such a steamy, secretive place, wide chestnut-lined avenues and broad harbors. It is by far the most cosmopolitan city we have visited. It is teeming out, but Don, being an old Navy officer, wants to see the harbor. We take off our shoes and simply run through the puddles, I, picking up my skirts, Don soaked and laughing, in our Shanghai translator Ma Yen Yen's straw lampshade hat.

Our last evening in China is subdued. We are all sad to leave each other. There were exchanges of hugs with Chen Mei, the distinguished and energetic Managing Director of the Summer Institute, and promises that we will all keep in touch.

I believe we will return to China someday. We have friends here. If we've learned anything, it is how small the world is and how universal we are as people in our emotions — in our desires and losses. "Keep in touch!" is the final shout. Everyone wants to keep the connection.

I think about a new play, about a translator whose name is something like Sun, about language and understanding, about confusion and clarity. I think about what Sun said, that during the revolution they were like refrigerators, just opened and closed, and how now China has opened its doors and we have gone in and somehow our lives are changed. I start to think about how I can transform the real incidents into a dramatic structure. Scenes start to run through my head — the initial welcome, digging through luggage for extra gifts, the classes at the Sleeping Buddha, the configuration of the Great Wall which incorporates the metaphor of the circularity, an American giving a valuable gift, it backfiring, a scene in the Passport office, a scene about bribery, early morning exercises in the park, the rigidity of the schedule "for tourists only," a scene in the Forbidden City, the question of how free China really is after the Cultural Revolution, and more. I think there is a play here. I went to China to teach, not to get a play, but that is what I seem to be returning home with.

Beijing Journals: April 1995

April 9, 1995

Sunday　　Going home. Going back to where it all began. It has been a journey of eight years since I went to China to teach. That time, I went with a small group of American Film professors; this time, I go alone. I am writing all of this on the airplane.

It was eight years ago that the original incident occurred which was the genesis for my play *A Small Delegation.* I hadn't gone to Beijing to find a play; however, the people and country had a spirit that captivated me, and I was hooked. In addition, something happened there that got me thinking, and for a playwright, that is the beginning of really being "hooked."

Now I'm returning for the performance of my play about China, in China. The first time, it was perhaps easier. There were no expectations. Now it is a re-visit, and you know how that is. I have no idea what the country will be like post-Tiananmen Square.

The first draft of the play was written in 1991, three and a half years after I taught in China, and written in Italy under a Rockefeller Fellowship. It was produced in Philadelphia in 1993 by Carol Rocamora and directed by Susan H. Schulman and designed by Ming Cho Lee. Now, it's 1995, and the play is going to China. It's kind of a miracle.

I think about the odyssey every work takes you on, the unexpected turns. It was always a dream to come back to China with this play. It feels, now, like a dream …

Shi Wei Jin, the Artistic Director of the China Youth Arts Theatre in Beijing, will meet me at the airport in three hours, together with Shi-Zheng Chen, my director, translator, and friend.

April 10, 1995

Monday   Arrival. It is now Monday evening. Somewhere we've gained a day. All time is lost. I think, in the shuffle, I may have had a drink of scotch for breakfast on the airplane in that place where night becomes morning. As we approach the lights of Beijing, my heart quickens. There is only one piece of sadness. It can only be the first time once. This time it will be different.

The airport is familiar — the disembarkation section, the quarantine section, the serious soldiers in khaki and red armbands, all with guns, and the sigh of relief after you pass through Security with your passport.

There are no carts for luggage to be found. The Beijing airport clerk tells me to be patient, and that more carts will probably come. Now I know I'm in China. The carts don't come, and I decide to drag the luggage myself. Then, somewhere in the baggage waiting process a conveyor belt with the entire luggage from the flight breaks down. The Chinese, in a more than patient and calm manner, fix it manually. Nobody shouts. All the passengers wait. Perhaps an hour passes. Patience ... Hsu. It will be fixed soon. And it is.

Beyond the arrival door, much like at JFK in New York, the throngs of welcoming family, friends, and limo drivers wait, waving signs. There is Shi-Zheng, and the handsome man with him must be Shi Wei Jin, the President of the Theatre. There is a woman with them. She turns out to be the actress playing the Chinese Translator. Of course, here in Beijing, all the actors will be Chinese, as will the production.

They have hired a small car, and we all pile in on the road to the hotel, taking a newly built highway. It is now close to midnight, and I have been traveling for more than twenty-four hours. But I have a surge of energy, just from the excitement of being here. We exchange the usual greetings — the thank yous, but there is nothing substantial yet. Shi Wei Jin and I begin then to exchange ideas, through Shi-Zheng, who is translating from somewhere in the middle of the back seat. We agree that our work is one half creativity and the other half politics: one hand the artist, the other the politician. If only we could just do the art. I wish I could speak Chinese so I could communicate directly with Shi Wei Jin, and not exhaust Shi-Zheng, our already overworked director, and now our translator, too.

We arrive at the Beijing Asia Hotel, which is beautiful. I it is also called the Jin Jiang Hotel. This was the same name of the hotel I stayed in the last time I was in China. Why are most hotels where Americans stay called the Jin Jiang? I will have to ask. No sooner am I in the hotel lobby registering than two men arrive. They are from the Beijing Film School. How do they just appear at midnight at my hotel? *That* is China. People simply turn up at the right time and place.

It seems I am to lecture tomorrow, the morning after arriving, at the Beijing Film School, and *only* for four hours. There will be a banquet in the evening. I am disappointed at not being able to spend the day with my actors at the rehearsal. Both Shi Wei Jin and Shi-Zheng assure me I must do the lecture, or it will be "bad politics." They tell me it is a good thing for an American to come and give something to China.

The professors from the Beijing Film School want the lecture to be about American Films of the Nineties. "But this is not my prepared lecture," I tell them. I will do the best I can. They ask me what videos I have brought. This is a touchy subject. "None," I say. How do you say, "wing it" in Chinese?

The actress who is playing Lu Xin in the play, the translator (the name is changed from the original name which I used in the American version) tells me she played the daughter in Marsha

Norman's 'Night, Mother when it was produced in Beijing. She also tells me there have been, to date, three American plays produced in China: Arthur Miller's *Death of a Salesman*, Marsha Norman's *'Night, Mother* and just last year, Amy Tan's *The Joy Luck Club.*

Now it is nearing 1:00 a.m. and everyone seems to be gathered in my room — Shi Zheng, Shi Wei Jin, the actress playing the translator, and another actress who has somehow showed up. She is introduced as the "Meryl Streep of China," and has also just lugged my bags up the stairs, despite my protests. I am told it is okay, "Kui." The two professors from the Beijing Film School are also in my room and have now taken off their coats. Are we all to sleep here? Later, the next morning, I wonder if I should have offered them a drink from the bar set-up.

Fading, I finally say, "Good night," Shi Zheng tells them something in Chinese that sounds longer than just "good night," and finally, everyone leaves. I then crawl happily into the lovely bed and the phone begins to ring in the next room. It continues ringing for thirty minutes. When I call the operator to explain the problem, she informs me that my phone is *not* ringing. I say that I know my phone is *not* ringing since I'm speaking on it. I try to explain the concept of the *next* room, the *adjoining* room, and the *other* room. It is now 2:00 a.m. and no use. We have a communications problem. Finally, I get dressed, go into the hall, and see what the next room number is, and a repair person is sent to disengage the phone. At 3:00 a.m. I happily fall asleep, looking forward to my first day in Beijing.

April 11, 1995

Tuesday   I slept in until 10:00 a.m. and feel refreshed. After breakfast, I take a walk through the streets. It is springtime in Beijing and all the trees are in bloom. The city is very changed since I was here eight years ago. The modern world seems to have caught up with Beijing. There are more tall buildings, construction everywhere, a new highway skirting past the old temples, large yellow taxi vans, and more cars now than bicycles. I miss the sound of bicycle bells as they warned the competing animals in the road, and the occasional diplomat's Mercedes. There are discos everywhere, and office complexes, and even malls, and every other person seems to be on a cell phone. In many cases, sit-down restaurants have replaced the old open-air stands where food was cooked and sold. In some ways it makes me sad because Beijing has lost some if its originality and become like any modern city.

Some things, however, are unchanged since eight years ago. There are the familiar sounds of the many Chinese dialects in the streets, live chickens and birds sold on corners, and parents with their one adorable child only (as allowed by the government) in tow. Today I saw one man in a blue Mao suit, and it was like seeing a leftover hippie from the sixties — a relic.

In the afternoon, I dutifully teach at the Beijing Film School. It is like re-visiting a scene, but now the students are more fashionably dressed, and their pagers are constantly ringing. "What is this?" I ask. "Pay no attention," one of the students tells me. "They are all drug dealers." The class laughs and I know it is a joke, so I laugh too. I manage through a lecture I am familiar with and am able to add sufficient facts from films of the nineties.

Afterwards, there is the inevitable banquet, presided over by the President of the Beijing Film School, President Leo, who urges me to drink the four different kinds of soup, including Turtle, otherwise the owner of the restaurant will be insulted and think their food is not good.

After dinner, I return to my hotel and fall asleep. When I wake up it is midnight, and still no call from Shi-Zheng about the next day's rehearsal schedule. Shi-Zheng has been in rehearsal all day, but I don't even know where he is rehearsing or the phone number of his hotel. What if he never calls? ... Patience, "hsu." Just when I am giving up hope and having a little cognac, he calls. It is 1:00

a.m., and rehearsal for the day has just ended. We make plans to meet for breakfast at 8:00 a.m., and then I am told to plan to rehearse all day and into the night. It sounds a little excessive, but the Chinese are hard workers, and I'm pleased that they care that much about my play. An old Clint Eastwood film, where he is a singer on his way to Nashville is on T.V. and I fall asleep to the American film.

April 12, 1995

Wednesday The day begins with breakfast with Shi-Zheng. He first explains why he is staying at a different hotel than I. It is a government hotel operated by the Chinese Army, and he tells me it will be a more "acceptable arrangement." It would not look good for him, born in Changsha, Hunan, to be staying at a fancy Westerner's hotel. He should be equal with the actors to make them feel at home. He then tells me diplomatically that they have had to make some changes in the script, "slight adjustments," since the Ministry of Culture is coming to the performance. For example, I cannot say that Mao is dead, even though he is. It would be okay for a Chinese to say it, but not a Westerner. It would be disrespectful. Shi-Zheng cites other examples. I understand diplomacy and the changes don't truly alter the meaning of the play, so I make them. "And another thing," he tells me, "in the script the bribe given to the Passport Officer in Act II by Mei Yen would be better given by the American." Why, or "weishenme"? I ask. Shi-Zheng explains that if an American gave the bribe it would be disrespectful, but if a Chinese person gave it, it would be acceptable, and therefore not cause the trouble needed for the plot. Since the bribe is the linchpin for the climactic action of the play, it better be the American in the play, Remy, who delivers the two bottles of Mai Tai in order to bribe the passport officer into giving Lu Xin a visa to come to America.

Rehearsal is in Shi-Zheng's hotel room at the Army Hotel, as the theater is in the process of rebuilding, I am told. Okay ...

I meet the actors and they seem perfectly cast. They also appear as actors anywhere, with all the nervous pre-rehearsal banter, and, instead of the All-American plastic cup of coffee, they carry their tea, their cha, brewed and brought from home in glass jars. The tea and cigarettes are a constant. "We smoke like chimneys," offers Wang Mei who plays Lili. She speaks, "a little American," she tells me.

Most of the actors are members of the company of the China Youth Arts Theatre, except for two who have been brought from a theater company in Shanghai, as many actors in Beijing are involved with the current year's project commemorating the Sino-Japanese war.[5]

Shi-Zheng then asks me to talk about the play and its central themes. I do. Shi-Zheng, of course, is doing double duty as both translator and director. I talk about the play being concerned with desire, the desire for love, freedom, and the desire to help, or be a "do-gooder"(as in Remy's case), which eventually causes the downfall of her Chinese friend. As in most dramas, few ever get what they want. Plays, after all, are not about happy people. That would be too boring. I promise the actors they will all find complete happiness ever after in the characters they play in their next productions, or, the sequel to this play — and only if it's a comedy.

We discuss the relationships of the characters to each other. The Chinese actors have the most difficulty in understanding the American characters in the play. This is the opposite problem we had with the American productions, where the American-born Chinese (ABC's) had difficulty with the Chinese characters they were playing.

"Why is Remy so pushy?" asks Wang Liu Yun, who plays Remy, the main American professor. I explain it is because she is insecure and wants to be liked. Also, it is selfish. It makes Remy feel good when she helps someone. In *A Small Delegation* her meddling leads to tragedy.

As we rehearse in the hotel room, I can see the Palace walls of the Forbidden City out the window. This is still like a dream … Rehearsal, however, is like all rehearsals everywhere, except that we are in a cramped Army Hotel in China.

During rehearsal, we go over the pronunciation of the English lines the actors need to say, as in the scenes with the lectures. The actress has trouble with the line, "I celebrate myself," from Walt Whitman's "Leaves of Grass."

We break for lunch, and go for what is called "a business lunch," but of such splendor as to be unimaginable. The actors have found a favorite restaurant nearby and keep returning to it. The thing in China, however, is *never* to empty your cup, because it will be refilled promptly; so, ten cups of tea later, I stagger out into the daylight. While we are having lunch, there is a good deal of flutter in the room, as Lu Xin is well known in Chinese films, and everyone in the restaurant recognizes the famous movie star.

At lunch, we talk some more about the script sitting around the table. I also learn from Shi-Zheng that the government is "investigating" the performance of the play, but probably there is "no problem," — Wei mentei. I am assured it is just business as usual, but I can see by his facial expression and the whispering back and forth that Shi Wei Jin is worried. Something must have happened at the Ministry in the morning while we were rehearsing.

Next, there is the matter of the "carriage money" to pay for the newspapers to show up. It is explained that this payment is for coming back and forth to the theater. It is travel money for the government officials and critics. In the old days, this payment was for the carriage to pick up the officials and the critics. The tradition has remained. I am assured everyone does it. You just slip a white envelope under the seat of the car when the press and the government officials arrive. In China, there is a surprise a minute. I agree to help with the "carriage money."

In the late afternoon, after some more rehearsals, I leave the actors on their own and go to the Forbidden City. I have been here before, but only with guides, not alone. Somehow I manage to get lost in the labyrinth of the Forbidden City, and maybe want to be lost from all responsibility for a few hours.

The ride home is hilarious. All the taxis at the Forbidden City seem to have broken meters. So, finally, I flag down a tricycle with a canopy, and the driver agrees to peddle me home for forty yuan — about five dollars. We travel through rush hour streets for hours, past buses, cars, around traffic circles, over bridges. (I find out later I had asked him to carry me halfway across the city!) It must make a funny picture, this woman in a black leather jacket, large sunglasses, wearing American cowboy boots, riding across the city in one of these open vehicles rather than the ubiquitous Mercedes cum driver for visiting Americans.

At night, Shi Wei Jin has arranged a banquet of seafood, exquisite crab and shrimp from his hometown in the South of China. It is the same hometown, he says, as Sun Yatsen. Shi-Zheng comments that, "all handsome men are from this town." Shi Wei Jin is pleased.

After dinner we go on to more rehearsal and more "cha." By 10:00 p.m. my eyes are closing and Shi-Zheng sends me home. They will rehearse until *they* are tired.

April 13, 1995

Thursday Shi-Zheng and I have a little ritual now. We meet for breakfast in the morning at my hotel, so we can get a good cup of coffee, and we discuss the day's rehearsal. The actors are beginning to relax. Shi-Zheng has told them this is not a serious drama, in order to eliminate any chance of melodrama. Some more scenes also need to be cut because of "questionable content." This directive comes from the Ministry of Culture or perhaps the actors themselves. It's hard to tell. I am told Chinese would never be so confrontational as in my play, for fear of retribution, but the confrontation scenes between the American professor and her Chinese translator are essential for the resolution of the play. What is becoming of the script? It seems only the bones are left, and I worry some the juice has been squeezed out to make it more "acceptable."

I take the morning off and write some postcards, then act like a tourist and go to the Friendship Store. The rows of cloisonné jewelry leave me empty. There's nothing I want here. I need to go back to my play.

The rehearsal process, at least, is familiar. The actors, like all actors, talk to themselves, memorize lines, run lines with each other, get impatient with themselves, work relentlessly, always want to do it just one more time, "zai." There are eight voices chattering at once. I recognize the sounds as the "music" of rehearsal. It wafts around me. I don't understand what they are saying, but do get the rhythms. Soon, I even believe I can make out what they're saying. I can tell by their emotions what scene we are in. I no longer need the director to tell me. At this point I realize they are new deep into the script now. No more fooling around, and no going back. They are almost off book.

The old woman, who I thought was the Stage Manager, is now coaching lines. Later it's explained that she was once a famous actress in China, and now is an acting coach *and* a stage manager. Okay. "Wei mentei."

At certain times, it seems everyone in the room is a director. Talk about democracy. Everyone offers line readings. In the States this would be considered mayhem. In China, all help is welcome in the theater. It's all considered family.

We have a quick dinner at the Army Hotel dining room. And then it's "Leila, leila, Leila," — let's get on with it. Back to rehearsal until 11:00 p.m., until we are all thoroughly worn out.

I think something like "imru" is "scene," because every few pages (the script is shorter in Chinese) the stage manager says "imru" something or other. Yes, I ask, and indeed "imru" does mean "scene." The most repeated word is "dui" or "exactly." So that's what Shi-Zheng has been saying all these years when we're on the phone and I'm speaking and he's listening on the other end, and repeating, "dui, dui, dui." I love the sound of it; I love the meaning "I'm listening." "Dui" is fast becoming my favorite word.

April 14, 1995

Friday   This morning I decide to hire a driver and go to see the Marco Polo Bridge. It is far away from Beijing. The driver speaks only Chinese, but we manage to communicate. He drives, asks me if it's okay, and I answer "dui, dui, dui," and he is pleased with himself.

On the way we pass much construction, as stone houses are being replaced with high-rise apartments. I am told later the "quaint hovels" are being torn down, and it is, in the end, good for the people of China. It is sad, however, to see the old go. Evidently these ancient stone buildings have no plumbing, so where is the beauty in it? Better, I am told, to keep it alive in memory.

The Marco Polo Bridge is one mile long and lined on either side with stone lions. The road across the bridge is paved with ancient cobblestones and smooth from wear. The river running under the bridge has long since gone dry. Marco Polo marveled, I am told, when he first saw this bridge on coming to China. It is still a marvel, albeit, lined now with souvenir stands and busloads of visiting schoolchildren. I buy two very old teapots and one Mao button.

After I return, I meet with some professors from the Beijing Film School and we discuss the possibilities of an exchange with New York University. Then, I go to the Beijing Hotel, a large monster of gentility. The hotel has the very old original part, and all the modern add-ons. The hotel has grown like some over-fertilized garden, in every which direction. We are to have a tech run-through here today. The play will be performed in a theater room called the Eden Garden. This is because the China Youth Arts Theatre is still "undergoing reconstruction." Okay …

Shi Wei Jin appears at the hotel, together with the actors. He looks exhausted. I later find out he has been up all night filling out papers that the Ministry of Culture is requesting. It is indeed life imitating art. In the play, the Passport Officer keeps demanding more and more papers.

So, Shi Wei Jin has been at the Ministry of Culture all morning getting the papers inspected and getting the production approved. I am told he has received the go-ahead. But if so, why does he look so dejected? At this moment, I have the feeling that perhaps the performance will be cancelled and that I should be prepared.

If Shi Wei Jin is in any jeopardy because of this play, I prefer we call it off right now. I tell this to Shi-Zheng, who assures me, "Wei mentei."

The Eden Garden Room is a knockout! It is the size of the Grand Ballroom at the Waldorf Astoria. It has an ample stage, and up to date lighting and sound systems. It also has floor to ceiling velvet draperies. The room must be three stories high. There are excellent reproductions of classical sculpture placed in the arches, like Venus de Milo and Michelangelo's Moses.

One of the actresses then recognizes the white-smocked waitress who brings us cha. It is a former classmate from high school. They embrace and exchange greetings. Wang Li Yun introduces her friend to the cast.

The tech rehearsal is like all tech rehearsals — stop and go, and creatively painful. That's why they call it "technical." Shi-Zhen has brought the original music track from our first production, as composed by Tan Dun. Tan Dun, who has now gone on to some renown in the States due to his opera *Marco Polo*, was originally one of Shi-Zheng's colleagues in the Beijing Opera. I hear the first bar of "Great Wall Music" and it is comforting — the mournful bells and the single flute.

The cast has to clear out by 5:00 p.m., as they serve dinner in the Eden Garden at that hour. Oh, the life of an actor. But it is a wonderful room and worth the musical chairs.

After the tech rehearsal, I learn why Shi Wei Jin is so wearied. Yes, we have approval to go on, but *only* for *one* performance, and it cannot be publicized in the newspapers. Great. One performance and no one will be there. Well, I can't show the actors I'm upset because it will upset them. Or perhaps someone must have told them the news by now. I am assured people will be there, like all the critics, because they now have their "carriage money." But what about a real audience? I am despairing, but this American playwright is not going to try and bargain with the Ministry of Culture and really endanger someone's life. Oh, and more news — this one performance must be, not as planned, in a week, but tomorrow, and a matinee. I gather they want to run us out of town as soon as possible. I no longer say Mao is dead in the play, and don't infer that the passport officer is at fault, and most of the negative references to the Cultural Revolution have been removed. What could be wrong now?

Frankly, even if they say the one performance cannot go on unless I make more changes, I am ready to walk away.

But the show will go on, and there is work. There are gifts to wrap for all the actors, and we have one last rehearsal, so there is no time to even consider the impact of the news. I have programmed myself to go with the flow here, but mostly, to do the best by the play, the actors, and the audience — if there is one.

That night, before our single grand performance, there is dinner with the American Embassy Cultural attaché, Gene Nowak. He agrees that Beijing is the toughest post he's had in terms of the political complexities. We agree, as Lu Xin says in the play, "China is a plate of sand." Things change minute to minute. We discuss the possibility of the Chinese cast coming to the U.S.; perhaps the Embassy will sponsor them. But, I won't hold my breath. There are many pieces of paper that would need to be signed between the thought and the reality.

There are indeed theaters in the U.S. that might consider an exchange with China. They would be theaters in large metropolitan areas with Asian or international populations, such as New York, Los Angeles, San Francisco, or Seattle. I promise to write those theaters when I return home.

I go back to my hotel and fall asleep by 9:30 p.m.

April 15, 1995

Saturday   Six-thirty a.m. The day dawns. Today is *it*. It is also Passover. It is also the anniversary of my mother's death — five years, or is it six? I wake up nervous, which is normal, but exchange it for excitement, by sheer force of will.

In the morning I skip the last rehearsal, and walk instead through the streets of Beijing for hours. There are some last minute gifts for people at home, and one for my forthcoming first grandchild. I buy a small cup with a picture of a pink pig on it, a "zhu."

The flight home the next day is at 9:40 a.m., and we must leave the hotel by 7:45, so I must pack today, after I return from shopping. The performance will start at 2:00 p.m. Not only are we scheduled down to one performance, but a matinee — the worst!

Before I leave my hotel there is a surprise phone call from none other than my original translator of eight years ago, Sun. She is back in Beijing from London and is coming to the performance, as is Bai Fengxi, the Chinese playwright I had met with on my first trip here. In the interim, I have seen Bai at the first International Conference of Women Playwrights in Canada. As for Sun, not a word has passed between us since she was admonished to cease and desist this friendship with the visiting American. I had stayed far away, as had she. But now, she would be seeing my play.

Armed with gifts for the cast, and a bottle of what else but Remy Martin cognac ("Remy" is, of course, the name of the American heroine in my play) for Shi Wei Jin.

It is D-Day.

At the massive Beijing Hotel, I have a glass of white wine and a tuna fish sandwich by myself, and then go backstage to wish the cast a good performance.

The play finally begins, and there is a large audience. I am relieved. Somehow the word has gotten out. So far, so good. I can follow every scene emotionally without being fluent in the language. The room is very quiet. This is good. The largest laugh comes when the American professor says, "I do not want to see Chairman Mao." Ironically, it is funnier than the original line, which was "I don't want to see the dead man in a glass box." I have, of course, rewritten the play to make it acceptable, made many cuts, and still, in a way, this is the most powerful performance yet. Why? "Weishanme?"

Is it perhaps because the script is pared down to the essentials? Is it because the Chinese cast has never performed such an intimate and confrontational play, and they are having a good time experimenting. Most Chinese plays are much less personal than *A Small Delegation*. By the last scene, when Remy realizes how she's unequivocally ruined Lu Xin's life, the actress is completely broken and in tears and it is real. This is a moment I've never seen realized before so truthfully. Wang Liu Yun has been doing a lot of Army or "public relations" films, so this play, she tells me, is more like Chekhov because the people are speaking "in their hearts." That's good enough for me.

After the performance, it is customary here for the playwright and director to meet with the critics. There are about twenty critics gathered from all over China, and they ask their questions and give their impressions one by one. This takes three hours, as all the comments here have to be translated, and at one point we have to move out of the Eden Garden, as they are about to set up for dinner. We move to the lounge of the Beijing Hotel.

Now my original translator, Sun, is doing most of the translating. It is like old times. The play is a triumph with the critics. This is important, I'm told, as they are key to the Government's approval.

The critics tell me they feel this is a landmark play, a breakthrough. They have never seen a play about both eastern and western cultures and their interactions before. They have never before seen the personal and intimate details of what people say when they are alone. They are used to a more public and presentational drama. How did an outsider see what the Chinese think they shield from even their own? How did *anyone* see it?

A Small Delegation, says the woman to my right, from *The Shanghai News*, is the first piece since Edgar Snow's *Red Star over China* to show a Westerner reflecting and comprehending the east. I've read every book on China except Snow's early book, and must read it when I return.

So words, like music, do travel. So the audience in China gets the play. What pleases me most is that the people of Beijing receive the play with affection and are moved, and that nothing was offensive. More than anything, I want to reach this audience, but with respect for the place I am returning to, where it all began — China.

We have a wonderful opening party/farewell banquet at our favorite restaurant. We all have too much Chinese vodka and we sing — songs from Beijing opera, songs from American movies, and we end with the theme song from *Casablanca*, "As Time Goes By" and everyone joins in.

The actors hope the production will go forward in Beijing. They also hope they can come to America and perform in repertory with an English speaking cast. Being in the theater, I am hopeful, but promise nothing. All I can hold in my hands is the small miracle we have somehow created.

Shi-Zheng and I came to China with this play, the place where it was born, and the place where much of the world's history was born. We were able to give it back to the Chinese people, who gave it all to me in the first place.

April 16, 1995

Sunday   I am in the air, on the way back from Beijing to New York. Mission accomplished, play presented. What a journey it continues to be with this play ... I have a few dollars left in Chinese money and decide to hold on to it. It will be good luck. Also, I get the feeling I will be returning to Beijing again. Now, home.

11

ADAPTING FROM FACT
AND FICTION

The subjects of our plays often choose *us*. Something we have read or heard or seen or dreamt, or a place we have traveled to, catches our imagination and doesn't let go, and we are off.

One of the things I've enjoyed about being a playwright is the varied canvas for writing projects it's afforded. I started out to be *just a playwright*, but there's no such thing. There's hardly a playwright I know who hasn't also written a film, written for television, composed poetry and short stories, attempted a novel, a children's book, magazine articles, and a nonfiction book, as well as done the book for a musical. Almost every playwright I know has authored some kind of adaptation, whether from fiction or fact.

In your career, the time will come when you are either commissioned or choose to adapt a novel, short story, or film for the stage. There will also be historical material that will attract you, or a book of nonfiction, perhaps a biography, or a real story that is brought to you or you read about, and you think it will make a good play.

The laws of public domain now covering a current piece of work are in effect for the entirety of the author's life plus seventy more years. For a chart regarding current 2005 rules of public domain, please refer to the end of this chapter.

If there is work you wish to adapt which is not in the public domain, it is recommended that you contact the author's agent and try to get permission to the rights.

Remember, also, that ideas or facts are not covered under laws of copyright. No one can own a fact; but the particularized expression of that idea *is* protected and is inviolate. In that way, all authors are covered for the exact placement of language in describing an idea — how one word follows the other.

In regard to the depiction of someone's life or a specific event, before you begin to write it is wise to get approval from the people involved or their agent. Although anyone is entitled to write a play about any public person, according to Ralph Sevuch, current director for the Dramatists Guild of America, litigious claims often do arise, arguing everything from defamation of character to the omission of an important event in the life of the person who is being depicted. Because you are not a journalist, and you are reconfiguring the real story in order to make it stage worthy, you are always better off clearly owning the rights.

If you are in doubt regarding your subject matter and your rights to the material, contact a lawyer who specializes in theater or copyright law, or contact the Dramatists Guild of America offices in New York and ask to speak to someone who can advise you on legal questions. Any playwright may join the Guild as an associate member and be entitled to the advice of the Guild in such matters.

Although it is more likely that you will need to adapt from fact in your career as a playwright, based on the number of existing dramatic adaptations, we'll discuss adapting from both fiction and fact. Perhaps adaptation from fact is the more popular form, as it allows for passions that originate with the author. There is a much larger opportunity for originality when adapting from fact, as challenging as adapting from fiction is. When adapting from fact, you do your research, do your interviews, and then it is up to you to formulate the story. There is more room to maneuver in an original play based on fact, whether it is based on a particular incident or a period in history that serves as background for your play. The genesis of the play is with you.

If you are adapting a short story or novel for the stage, what you want to do the following:

- After reading the novel or short story, make a step-by-step outline of the plot.
- Next, list every character.
- Then, on a piece of graph paper, plot out the rising action of the short fiction or novel. What is the major dramatic incident?
- Where will you choose to start? Is it a place already described in the novel or will you be constructing a new opening scene?
- Go through all "Fifty Questions to Ask When Writing a Play," Chapter 3, determining which questions are answered in the piece of fiction as it is, and where the holes are.
- In rereading the book, what material will you choose to exclude? Why?

Then:

- Decide how you may choose to change the plot in order to increase the dramatic tension.
- Decide how many of the real characters you plan to keep, considering practicalities. Which characters will you preserve and why? Will you cut some characters? Which ones? Will you merge some of the characters? How?

- Construct a new plot outline, incorporating *your* choice of characters and plot line.
- Know approximately where you want to end the play, but wait until the actual writing of the play so that your characters can lead you to the end.

Understand that in some instances a piece of fiction may be adaptable for the stage while keeping generally quite faithful to the original text. If so, you are fortunate, but you do want to ask: Why adapt this particular piece to the stage if it has already been written for the printed page and even for film? What does the stage do for a piece that few other mediums can accomplish, given the changing audience and performance every evening? I always think of the stage as a musical composition, with each concert — conductor, location, and orchestra adding to the life of that piece.

Although it is much more common to adapt a novel into film because of the availability of location and scope in a film, as well as the camera's ability to concentrate on the persona by the use of close-ups (thereby possibly utilizing the interior passages in a novel), there are several examples of successful adaptations of novel and short story to stage. There are many more novels adapted into musicals for the stage, but here we are only discussing fiction into straight drama. Successful stage adaptations of fiction include Edward Albee's brilliant adaptation of Vladimir Nabokov's *Lolita*, Ruth and August Goetz's *The Heiress*, suggested by the Henry James novel *Washington Square*, and the recent fine adaptation by Peter Parnell of John Irving's novel, *The Cider House Rules*. Perhaps one of the best classic examples of a novel adapted for the stage is Steinbeck's *The Grapes of Wrath*.

The Grapes of Wrath, a Pulitzer Prize–winning novel, written by John Steinbeck and published in 1939, tells the story of a displaced farm family from Oklahoma who travels to California in search of a "promised land." They only want to work and live in dignity as a family, by Ma Joad. Their arduous journey to California, punctuated by death and desertion, is extended by travel between the migrant labor camps, while attempting to find meaningful and satisfying work. The family continues to suffer indignities, harassment, and outright persecution by corporate entities and local law enforcement, and they survive day-to-day, doing "what you have to do." Their spirit is sustained by an enduring belief in the connection between "common folk" for mutual support and benefit.

This basic story of a migrant farm family from the Dust Bowl in the midst of the Great Depression resonates through succeeding generations as a great American novel, and was a significant reason for Steinbeck's receiving the Nobel Prize for Literature in 1962. The novel was made into a prize-winning film in 1940, scripted by Nunnally Johnson, directed by John Ford, and starring Henry Fonda as Tom Joad, the protagonist in the story and the film. The theater director, Frank Galati, adapted the novel for stage, and the Steppenwolf Theatre Company of Chicago first presented it in 1988. There were subsequent productions of the play at the La Jolla Playhouse in La Jolla, California, and at the Royal National Theatre of Great Britain, both occurring in 1989. In 1990, the play was produced on Broadway, directed by Frank Galati, and received a Tony Award as best play in that year.

In his book *The Grapes of Wrath: Trouble in the Promised Land*, Louis Owens explains the of biblical parallels in four of the five layers claimed by Steinbeck:

> On one level it is the story of a family's struggle for the survival in the Promised Land. On another level it is the story of a people's struggle, the migrant's. On a third level it is the story of a nation, America. On still another level, through ... the allusions to Christ and those to the Israelites and Exodus, it becomes the story of mankind's quest for profound comprehension of his commitment to his fellow man and to the earth he inhabits.[1]

This linear and profound novel presents a clear challenge to the playwright, as the novel employs an unusual presentation of hard-hitting general information in chapters that alternate with longer chapters on the Joad family's struggle. These chapters act as a kind of Greek chorus to underline and expand the struggles and challenges of the migrant men and women. In fact, music has a prominent place in the novel and the Saturday night dance at the Weedpatch Camp is the setting for a major confrontation. Frank Galati incorporates much of to story in song and music that separates, and provides transition for, the scenes involving the Joad family. Music is also used to define and reinforce the action on stage; for example, the recurring musical theme that represents the engine of the Joad's dilapidated truck.

This illustrates the premise that a theatrical play is more than just a sequence of speeches. The music, sound effects, setting, scenery, and costumes all contribute to the telling of the story. The playwright needs to consider all of these effects and identify, in the script, those elements necessary to propel the story and action forward. As Frank Galati points out in an Author's Note in the Dramatists Play ssevice edition of the script, the Steppenwolf Ensemble once performed this play on a bare stage. Galati goes on to describe Kevin Riddon's design, in which a single long trough of water represented the Colorado River, a stream that floods the box-car camp, and the torrential rain at the end of the second act. Despite the simplicity of this device, the audience never lost track of the story; instead, their imaginations were engaged.

The process for adapting a novel to stage starts with an understanding of the multiple layers of the story and the character motivations, both physical and emotional. This informs the subsequent choices for dramatization of scenes to provide the spine of the play and emotional development of the characters.

The playwright must hold tight to the emotional reins of the story, and learn as much as possible about the circumstances surrounding the novel, including the setting in time and place, author's commentary, if any, and possible insights by reviewers. In the end, the playwright must make choices in eliminating material and, possibly, entire scenes, or revising the sequence and actions of the novel. This is inherent as a novel often enjoys the luxury of length, description, repetition, and internal thoughts, and may introduce characters and events that enhance the story and provide supporting elaboration, but may not be essential to the emotional spine of the story. They may, in effect, be more decoration for the script tree than it needs.

Some examples from Galati's script illustrate this point. In the first specific chapter of the novel, Tom Joad hitches a ride with a truck driver on the way home from prison where he has been released on parole from a seven-year sentence for killing a man. This introduces Tom and provides background for the times (the driver is violating company rules by picking up a rider). In the second specific chapter, Tom walks up the dusty dirt road toward home and finds Jim Casey, the preacher (now inactive, but still in demand later) sitting under a tree. This introduces Casey and Joad family background and they leave together toward the old homestead. In the film version, the action starts with a bus stopping along a highway, and Tom exits, beginning his walk up the dirt road. In the play, the action begins with Casey playing a little harmonica and then singing a church hymn. Tom enters the scene and the two begin the dialogue. Eliminating the scene with the truck driver does not diminish the initial thrust of the story, which is captured in the scene between Tom and Casey. The truck driver never appears again in the novel, but Casey plays a major role in the story.

In the adaptation from the novel to the script, adjustments to specific actions are very often necessary to streamline the flow without losing the emotional thread. You should examine the texts of *The Grapes of Wrath* yourself, and decide if you agree with the choices and changes made, to determine if the play maintains the emotional backbone of the original story.

In beginning any adaptation from fiction for stage, we are ultimately forced to select what and who will stay, who will be let go, and who will be added. The process is similar to the rewriting process in that you are concerned with ensuring there are clarity, conflict, confrontation, resolution, tension, drama, and ultimate change in your adaptation. Ultimately you are looking at the way the author told the original story and deciding how *you* want to tell the story. Remember that your adaptation is always "based on." You, the playwright, make a decision either to be fairly faithful to the text or to reimagine it. Always try to see things in a new pattern. As writers, we should always be trying to stretch. It's known as flexing your writing muscles.

The process of adapting from fact is a more complex and, to me, a more exciting prospect. Because we cannot always write solely out of our own bellies and hearts, there comes the time when we yearn for the framework and support of available facts, pulling them together like so many pieces of railroad ties. Sometimes, in doing the research, it is as if you were sifting through gold and fashioning from it a rich mosaic or linear story. It's as if you are the sculptor, given the materials, and you must give the shape. In writing a play that originates only out of your own imagination, no one supplies the material. In an adaptation, you mine the material.

Playwright Peter Parnell was commissioned by the Mark Taper Forum in Los Angeles to write *QED*, based on the life of physicist Richard Feynman. Feynman had written three books that were edited by his close friend Ralph Layton. After Feynman died, Layton wrote his own book about their friendship based on events when Feynman was already quite ill. When actor Alan Alda read Layton's book, he was hooked, and Parnell was asked to write his play with Alda in mind, based on the book.

In an interview in *The Dramatist*, Parnell says:

> I started dramatizing the book as well as I could, with lots
> of scenes and jumps in time, which was interesting because

Feynman was a quantum physicist, but it didn't work, primarily because Feynman didn't have a lot of secrets or regrets. The one thing that did make sense to me was to focus on the last years of his life, when he struggled with cancer. I thought that seeing a brilliant mind dealing with mortality would be interesting. That was the one theme running through every draft. Well they weren't drafts but plays — one with eight characters, one with six, one with two. In one I even invented a young physicist for Feynman to work with.

With each draft we read, Alan got more and more depressed. He loved the character and what I was doing, but he knew we weren't getting to the heart of it. After about six drafts of the play and several years of working on the play, between TV series and other projects, I was about to give up when I finally thought "Why don't I just see what happens if I have Alan alone."[2]

The resulting one-man show was a combination of Feynman's words and Layton's words and the playwright's words, and its success has to do with Parnell's brave and right choice to incorporate a complex life into the one major character, and the choice of the concentration of the last part of his life as the center of the play. It is about selection, and as you can see, perseverance. The excitement is often in the process of figuring out how to tell the story.

Authors, from Mark Twain to Tennessee Williams to Oscar Wilde to Lillian Hellman and Mary McCarthy, are often the subjects for stage plays. One can only hope that our lives are equally filled with drama. In fact, I have rarely met a boring playwright. Controversial? Yes. Flamboyant? Yes. Egotistical? Yes. Competitive? Yes. Filled with demons and anxieties? Yes. Well traveled? Yes. Complicated love lives? Yes. Inveterate storytellers? Yes. Adventurers? Yes. Alive? You bet! Dramatic? Absolutely! Some of my best friends? Forever!

In addition to biographical plays, there are the documentary plays that deal with real people and the dramatization of their words. Recently, writers Jessica Blank and Erik Jensen pieced *The Exonerated* together from interviews, which enjoyed a long, successful, and astonishingly moving production at the 45 Bleecker Street Theatre in New York, under the auspices of the Culture Project. Their subjects were men who had been on death row and were eventually exonerated.

In gathering the material for the play, the authors felt it was important to preserve their actual words as much as possible. They describe the process of gathering the interviews, court material, letters and poetry and other supporting documents, and then chipping away at the whole, as sculptors, so that the remaining play represented the question they were probing: What could have gone wrong in a court system that incarcerated a group on death row who were not guilty?

They describe their process in the same article in the *Dramatists Guild Quarterly*, as interviewed by Ralph Sevuch of the Guild:

> When we first got the idea, we did research and tracked down about forty people who spent from two to twenty-two years on death row for crimes they didn't commit before being released by the court.
>
> After we transcribed those interviews, since we're both actors, we called up our actor friends and started reading the transcripts and editing the material by ear.
>
> We had thousands of pages of material, but knew a ninety-minute intermissionless play was the right format. To stay in that timeframe and tell the stories fully, we had to cut the number of people to six. You meet each person, hear about their arrest and conviction, see their court trial, visit them in prison, and then hear about their release and their life afterward. So there

is a linear line for each, but the stories are interwoven. In the structure of the play they're interconnected.

In compressing such an enormous amount of narrative into a very small time, particularly a legal narrative with evidence that's so complex, we had to boil each case down to its essence.

The problem was there wasn't much tension, even though it's a life and death play; but we very quickly realized that the tension comes from the audience as they follow the stories of these exonerated, who've altogether spent about one hundred years on death row.[3]

So, in adapting from fact, the dramatist's tasks are doubled. Not only do you have to select and condense the material you gather, as well as put it into a timeframe, but in addition you have to attend to all the usual rules of any play, including character, dialogue, conflict, confrontation, escalating plot, and an organic ending. In one form, writing a purely original play, you are creating the pieces as you write. In adaptation, you first collect the pieces and, then, shape them into a play.

Shirley Lauro's *A Piece of My Heart* and Emily Mann's *Still Life* are two examples of documentary plays that came out of the Vietnam era. Shirley Lauro's play, which opened at the Actor's Theatre of Louisville in 1991 and premiered in New York at the Manhattan Theatre Club, was based on interviews with nurses who served in the Vietnam War and on a set of interviews recorded in the book of the same name by Keith Walker. Walker interviewed twenty-six American women who had served in Vietnam. In Lauro's play, she chose to tell six of the stories, using the actual women's words in some places and her own in others. Lauro preserves the stories depicted in the initial interviews, but transposes, compresses, and shapes them to make a wholly exceptional and moving play, one that is among the most frequently produced in this country.

Emily Mann's *Still Life* was first presented at the American Place Theatre in New York in 1981. The play was based on Mann's own interviews with three people she met in Minnesota in the summer of 1978, and much of the text is taken directly from these interviews, including an ex-Marine Vietnam vet and his wife.

Still Life is published by Dramatists Play Service, and the following passage is from the end of the play:

> *(Mark points to his photograph, an orange, a broken*
> *egg, with a grenade in the center on a dark background.*
> *Also some fresh bread, a fly on the fruit. From far away*
> *it looks like an ordinary still-life)*

Mark: My unit got blown up. It was a high contact. We got hit very, very hard. The Marine Corps sends you this extra food, fresh fruit, bread, a reward when you've had a heavy loss. What can I say? I'm still alive — my friends aren't. It's a still-life. I didn't know what I was doing.

I was in the theater at that first production. I recall, as the play ended there was not a sound in the audience for a long time. It seemed as though the silence after the conclusion of the play was forever. Up to that point I had never seen the likes of it in the theater. The audience was a complete puddle. Emily Mann was seated behind me, tears streaming down her face, but very quietly. Then, the applause started. It is one of the most honest plays I have ever witnessed, and Emily has gone on to write several highly political plays based on fact, including the award-winning *Execution of Justice*, based on recorded interviews and the transcript of the trials from the assassinations of George Moscone and Harvey Milk. Although *Still Life* was based on the author's own interviews, Emily Mann was also faced with the same task as Shirley Lauro in condensing the material and reshaping it into an affecting drama.

Guantanamo, Nine Parts of Desire, and *The Laramie Project* are representative of contemporary documentary plays. *Guantanamo,* by Victoria Brittain and Gillian Slovo, is based on spoken evidence from prisoners at the U.S. prison camp in Guantánamo and was based on an initial idea commissioned by Nicholas Kent of the Tricycle Theatre in London. In the play the authors weave personal stories, legal opinions, and political debate. The speeches by the prisoners themselves take the forms of direct address, direct narrative, or letters home. The prisoners, in caged cubicles in the production I saw by the Culture Project, never interact, emphasizing the isolation. What the authors accomplished with this dramatization was the personalization of the prisoners, or "the others."

Heather Raffo, who is an Iraqi-American, wrote *Nine Parts of Desire,* based on a decade of interviews with Iraqi women. The interviews took place between 1993 and 2003, so the play deals mainly with the consequences of thirty years of Saddam Hussein's repressive regime, and the suffering of the first Gulf War, leaving us to contemplate the added devastation of America's current war in Iraq. The play gives us an intimate look at nine vastly different Iraqi women who struggle not only with the burden of tradition but the anguish of war and survival guilt. Raffo took the title of the play from a book by Australian reporter Geraldine Brooks, who in turn quotes from the Koran, "God made desire in ten parts and gave nine to women." The proverb is often cited as justification for the cloistering of Islamic women. *Nine Parts of Desire* premiered at the Edinburgh Fringe Festival in 2003, went on to the Bush Theatre in London, and opened off-Broadway in New York in 2004.

Moises Kaufman and Stephen Belber's *The Laramie Project* is about a specific event: the death of Matthew Shepard in Laramie, Wyoming. Matthew Shephard was a twenty-one-year-old student at the University of Wyoming who was kidnapped in 1998, severely beaten, and left to die tied to a fence in the middle of the prairie. The evidence was that he had been assaulted because he was gay.

Kaufman, Belber, and members of the Tectonic Theatre Project visited Wyoming just a month after the murder. They went out with tape recorders and asked the people in the area to talk about anything they wanted to and for as long as they wanted. Some people talked about the gay angle, or the Catholic angle, or the character of the two boys accused, or the lifestyle of Laramie itself. The location became a character in the story in its own right.

The group made a total of six or seven trips to Laramie, not really sure that they had the material for a play. In writing the play the authors used mostly verbatim text taken from interviews and court transcripts. Because there was, at the time of the writing of the play, a gag order on the two suspects, some material central to the play had to be omitted. They were able to get interviews, however, from families and friends of the suspects; but they were never able to get them to sign a release as they believed the play would be nothing but a piece of gay propaganda, so the material from those interviews was not available for the play. The result is a tapestry woven by the authors of the effects of a tragedy on any community. If there is a question in the play, it is, "How could this happen here? Could this happen anywhere?"

It is of interest, in light of the recent elections in the United States, that the authors have sometimes been criticized, despite their good intentions, for putting the "locals" under a spotlight. There is a tendency in the play to look at the unsophisticated characters in the community as "those people who don't get it." When we look at the results of the 2004 U.S. election and the majority of red states that voted for George W. Bush, and the intellectuals who voted for Kerry, *The Laramie Project* and its point of view deserve reexamination.

Experientially, I have written two plays that required extensive research. The genesis and process of the first, *A Small Delegation*, is described in Chapter 10. This play had its beginnings in a real incident that happened while I was teaching in China. The characters in the play are all amalgams of real people and the plot of the play is imagined. The play required a year of research, as I was dealing with the post–Cultural Revolution period, and as such, needed to know the history of the Cultural Revolution and the events leading up to it. Before I could begin the play I interviewed several dozen people who had lived through the Cultural Revolution, tried to remember conversations I had had while I was in China, and read every book I could find — be it novel, short fiction, nonfiction, or poetry — that dealt with the Cultural Revolution, including a couple of general histories of China. By the time I started the play, I knew enough to be able to present a faithful portrait of China in the late 1980s, and one that continues in relevance. The research books on what I call "The China Project" take up two shelves on my bookcase.

Currently I am working on a play about South Africa. Act I takes place during the apartheid period, from 1948 to 1986. Act II begins in 1986, continues through the election of Nelson Mandela as president (1994), and culminates with the hearings of the Truth and Reconciliation Commission (1998–2000).

The play was generated by the story of a South African woman, Helen Lieberman, and her struggles together with a group of Xhosa and Zulu women to form a grassroots organization called Ikamva Labantu. These Xhosa words mean "the future of a nation" or "the mending of a nation" and that is the title of the play.

The story, as told to me, presented a challenge, as it took place over sixty years and involved hundreds of people and their stories; the material, however, was filled with drama and dealt with some of the same political issues I confronted in *A Small Delegation.*

It all started with a friend in the New York University community, Dean David Finney. He was sponsoring a series of lectures on South Africa, including one by Antjie Krog, the South African author of *Country of My Skull*, an account of the work of the Truth and Reconciliation Commission. Since Antjie was a playwright, he suggested I might be interested in hearing her speak. But he had something additional in mind.

Following the lecture there was a small dinner for Antjie and some South African scholars, and Dave whispered to me, "Sit next to Professors Jacqueline Jaffe and Rolf Wolfswinkel. I think Jacqueline has a story that might make a good play." At dinner she told me the story, and I was captivated.

Professor Jaffe, a scholar of English literature at NYU, had been on leave doing a project in South Africa, and during her visit, she came across a story of a remarkable group of women. While in South Africa she also fell in love with Professor Wolfswinkel, a leading scholar in Holocaust studies at the University of South Africa in Cape Town. Eventually the two married and he moved his career to NYU. Rolf had lived in Cape Town during the entire apartheid period, as well as during the Truth and Reconciliation Commission hearings, and proved to be a valuable resource for the material I eventually was working with.

How did it all come together? First, arrangements were made for me to meet Helen Lieberman in New York and get her approval. We connected immediately; Helen gave her blessings, with one caveat. The play should not be solely about her but about the women who worked with her. I reassured her and the research began.

Within a few months I was off to Cape Town where I stayed with Helen and her family and was put into contact with dozens of people who had been active in organizing against apartheid. Since Helen is still working actively in post-apartheid South Africa, I was also able to follow her around every day and make many trips to the outlying townships as well as study many of the programs Helen had established. These included AIDS centers, programs for the elderly, preschool programs, houses for orphans, programs for the blind, sports programs, and a small factory where a couple of dozen women, many disabled, sewed dolls and animals that are sold around the world to raise funds to help the thousands still in need in the townships.

While in Cape Town, I recorded more than fifty interviews, adding these to some original archival interviews done by Jacqueline Jaffe. Then I interviewed people who had been actively involved in the apartheid regime as well as those who were part of the Truth and Reconciliation Commission.

Armed with the interviews, I returned home, transcribed them, and then began the reading. As in the play about China, I gathered every book I could find on the history of South Africa, personal journals from the apartheid period, including Nelson Mandela's from Robben Island, books and documentaries about the Truth and Reconciliation Commission, including Alex Boraine's *A Country Unmasked*, and books about international truth commissions, including Patricia Hayner's *Unspeakable Truths*.

In addition I worked with materials at the Library of Congress as well as documents filed with the South African Courts of Law. As I read, I summarized the major points from each document on large index cards.

Six months later, I returned to South Africa to complete all the interviews. I finally started the organization and writing of the play a year later, at the Rockefeller Institute's Villa Serbelloni in Bellagio, Italy, where I was in residence in May 2004. Two boxes of notes and two boxes of books were mailed beforehand, ready for me upon my arrival.

At this point, some kind of structure started to take shape. The first thing I did was draw a horizontal historical time line on large sheets of white paper and tape it to the walls of my study. Next I decided who my main characters would be and which characters were composites of the real people I interviewed.

Next I decided to trace the six main characters' stories, based on all the interviews, and often combining several true stories. To do this, I went through all the interviews and highlighted the major points of each interview. Now I was ready to write monologues for each of the six main characters. Those initial monologues would eventually be used in the play, in various scenes.

The next task was marking the individual stories as they happened along the time line. I knew that I would piece the play together like a mosaic, starting with Helen, and then trace how each person came into her life until they all combined to make the whole story. I was looking for a common thread that attracted all of them to Helen and the work she was doing. And I found it. They all said they couldn't bear to live with the atrocities of apartheid any more. They had to do something.

Then I color coded each character and highlighted the research relevant to each character. Then I color coded certain time periods and went through all the interviews and research again, highlighting the information corresponding to those periods with matching colors. Then I outlined Acts I and Act II of the play, and I was ready to begin.

For a long time I had heard the first line of the play in my head. It would be Helen's and she would begin: "This story is not about me. Get that straight. Every woman was a Mama to Africa." With that I was off and wrote the first scene that was the actual genesis of the story, with Helen on the steps of Groote Schuur Hospital with a dead black baby. From there the characters took over and began to write the scenes for me, sometimes following the outline, other times not. I knew what the last scene of the first act would be and I knew what the very last scene in the play would be. At Bellagio, I completed Act I, and am currently completing Act II.

The process is like piecing together a giant jigsaw, and the joy of fitting all the pieces together into a coherent and moving story has been nothing short of thrilling. The people and their stories is what this play is all about, and what any good adaptation for the stage encompasses. All our struggles are heroic, and to be able to touch any one of them in your lifetime as a playwright is a gift.

This lecture was delivered to a graduate class in Adaptation at New York University's Tisch School of the Arts, Spring 2005. It has been slightly revised for inclusion in this book.

Copyright Duration and Renewal at a Glance	
Date of Copyright	Copyright Duration
Published or registered before 1923*	Copyright expired. Work is in public domain.
Published or registered 1923–1963	28-year initial term from date of copyright; 67-year renewal term if renewal registration filed. Term is 95 years. If renewal registration not filed, copyright has expired.
Published 1964–1977	28-year initial term from date of copyright; 67-year automatic renewal term. Term is 95 years. Renewal is optional.
Unpublished and unregistered works	Life plus another 70 years. If work remains created before 1978 unpublished, work cannot expire before Dec. 31, 2002. If work is published by Dec. 31, 2002, copyright cannot expire before Dec. 31, 2047, no matter when author died.
Created on or after January 1, 1978	Life plus another 70 years. No renewal required.
Joint works created on or after January 1, 1978	70 years after the death of the last surviving author. No renewal required.
Anonymous, pseudonymous works, and works-for-hire created on or after January 1, 1978	95 years from publication or 120 years from the year of creation, whichever comes first.
*Please note that unpublished and unregistered works created before 1978 cannot expire until, at least, December 31, 2002.	

Three Exercises in Adapation

1. Choose a piece of fiction that has been adapted for both film and stage. Compare the original version with the two adaptations. Does one stand out as better than the others? Why?

2. Take one week's worth of daily newspapers and find one story in them that you are interested in adapting. What kind of research would be required in order to adapt the story? Does the prospect excite you? Then you know you're on to something!

3. Choose an event — current or historical — that had always excited your curiosity. Remember that most adaptations based on fact involve the writer in solving a mystery. You are often writing to find out why or how something happened. First, isolate the questions you want to answer, and then go to those resources that may provide answers. In this day and age, research is simplified ... just google to get yourself started.

12

THE DO'S AND DON'TS OF PLAYWRIGHTING: WHAT I KNOW TO BE TRUE

Recently, I sat on a playwriting panel whose task was to choose grant recipients. There were over a hundred entries, and we were asked to rank each dramatic writer. At the end of the day, it was clear who the frontrunners were. I thought about those writers who did not make it to the top ranks. What were the things they had in common? I thought about those qualities that separated the more and less successful playwrights and identified the factors that ruled out many plays, starting with the most common mistakes:

1. Excessive verbiage — just plain overwriting.
2. Lack of originality and predictability.
3. Lack of clarity. What is this play about?
4. Terrible dialogue. Banal, trite, flat, generic, and not particular to each character.
5. Lack of complexity.

6. Lack of conflict and dramatic incident.
7. Underdeveloped characters.
8. Underwriting — not exploring the possible explosive moments in the play.
9. Lack of focus — trying to write ten plays at once.
10. An early promising draft. Laziness. Not buckling down and doing another draft.

Those plays that *did* make it to the top tier, varied as they were in subject matter, did share the following common characteristics:

1. Originality — a fresh idea no one had ever seen before.
2. Selectivity. There was no fat in the play.
3. Excellent dialogue. Dialogue particular to the character — individual voices.
4. Clear focus and themes.
5. Relevant contemporary subject matter delivered with passion — even when put in a historical context.
6. Energy!
7. Major identification with at least one character and his journey.
8. The ability to move the reader/audience.
9. Interest in the story — you are investing in finding out what would happen next.
10. Theatricality — a play that could be successfully staged.

The process of reviewing playwriting applicants on various panels and over many years brings me to the following conclusions about the dos and don'ts of playwriting.

There is always the odd play that pays no attention to any rules and flies off the page and stage, and that's important to keep in mind. If I were to urge anything, it would be to be true to your initial vision, instinct, and passion, and run with it. That, in the end, makes for originality.

My first full-length play was called *Flying Horses*. Its premiere production was at the University of Montana where I was a playwright-in-residence. The play was about a doctor who was a perfectionist and found something wrong with every item in his household. He had returned twenty refrigerators, twenty-five television sets, and thirty mattresses. The family, in fact, slept on a mattress still encased in plastic, in case it had to be returned. In his practice, the doctor, true to character, ran every test conceivable, regardless of the cost, and, on every patient, in order to detect the smallest imperfection. When one of the doctor's patients dies of questionable causes (perhaps one of the tests given), the doctor is called before a board of colleagues and his license to practice is revoked. The play was an absurdist comedy with a serious ending. I thought, "If someone returned everything in their household, they would finally be left with nothing."

So, in that first Montana production, and in accordance with the script, in the second act, while the action continues upstage, two moving men in white uniforms are deconstructing the entire set.

When the play was next done, the director/dramaturg told me that the second act did not make any sense. He told me it was not real. He said no one could identify with the action. And so, being a young playwright, I dutifully rewrote the second act and made it a tidy, realistic play. I sanitized it. Long after the production I showed the new script to my friend and colleague Zelda Fichandler who asked, "But what happened to that wonderful second act where the set is deconstructed?" I had erased all the originality from my own play. There is something valuable about our first instincts before we censor ourselves.

For the record, these are the general do's for a playwright:

1. Create engaging characters. They must be real. The playwright must write "as if" in the shoes of the character emotionally. Be honest in creating each character's psyche. You must know what each character is feeling (as well as saying) at every moment of the play. Draw an emotional line for each character through every scene.

2. The audience must care about the characters. What does it mean to "care" about a character? It presumes we have a vested interest in what happens to him or her and we identify with the challenges and misfortunes of the character in the progression of the play.

3. Show the audience the characters' weaknesses, their vulnerability, and how that affects their choices. Our choices are our morality, and are represented on stage by our actions.

4. Something must be in danger of happening! Then, that thing, or something even larger and unexpected must happen. Explore your character's hidden fears in the face of these dangers.

5. Be absolutely clear. The play can only have one spine, and all the action must root from that spine.

6. Edit ruthlessly, within each sentence, each speech, and each scene.

7. Always keep the action moving. If you can get through a hand's-width of dialogue without anything happening, start cutting! While the occasional speech that comes out of an emotional moment is acceptable and even necessary, density of conversation does nothing but obscure the action and lose your audience.

8. If you are writing a comedy, it should always stem from reality and find its own way to lunacy.

9. Give your characters needs. Then, put an obstacle in the way of them achieving these needs. That's your conflict.

Without conflict there is no drama. Then, make sure that your main character confronts the conflict.

10. Make it difficult for your main character to walk away from this conflict. The more difficult it is, the greater the tragedy.

11. Every scene has to be about something specific. Give each scene a title that reflects its central action and its major emotion. If your scene is not about something, either you don't know what the characters want or you don't have the characters' voice nailed.

12. The more specifically you write about your experience, the more universal your work becomes.

13. Attend to the needs of your characters as delineated by sociologist Abraham Maslow and his Hierarchy of Needs. Start with our basic physiological needs: food, shelter, sex. Move up to safety and security, then ego status and esteem, and then move to the highest level of realization and self-actualization. What are your characters missing? The missing elements are often precisely what your characters will go after. They constitute desire.

14. A play must have a beginning, middle, and end. The beginning should be rapid, the middle should build in excitement, and the end should complete or suggest the completion of the play's promise, which runs quickly from the high point in the action.

15. Do make the chain of events clear. You should be able to trace cause and effect throughout the play.

16. Identify the turning points. These are not often the great moments — they are often concealed in occurrences seemingly so trivial that they pass unobserved. "There is a tide in the affairs of men which taken at the flood leads on to fortune. Omitted, all the voyages of their life are

bound in shallows and in miseries" (Shakespeare's Julius Caesar).

17. Dare to think big.

18. Have the courage to tell the truth about the way things are, or the way things could be. Peter Handke, the Austrian author, said, "Few men have the courage go see the truth, and even fewer, the courage to tell it."

19. Go where they want your play and want to do it. That means the artistic directors and producers "get" your play and you do not have to plead for approval. When you know you are wanted from the outset, it propels you into your work and gives you the willingness to listen to what those people have to say about your play, and to do the hard line rewriting before going into rehearsal and during rehearsal.

20. Make deadlines with yourself. Mark them down in your diary. Be firm. A good trick is to set up a reading for a future date. Engage actors you know. Set it up in your own home or a friend's. Promise the scripts delivered to the actors one week prior to the reading. Invite some trusted colleagues. You will make the deadline.

21. Rewrite! Rewrite! Rewrite! After the first draft and a trusted colleague has read it, after the first public reading, after the first workshop, after the first production, prior to the next production, prior to publication, rewrite until you are certain the script is as good as you can get it. Then, like Moses, open the gates, and let the play go forth into the promised lands.

For the record, these are the general don'ts for a playwright:

1. Don't write a play because you think certain subjects are currently popular, or because you think a particular subject will be of interest to a producing director.

2. Don't write a play only because you think it will be "important."

3. Don't be self-indulgent, saying every clever thing that comes to mind.

4. Don't sit down to write the play until you have identified the individual voices for each character, whether through biography or through written exercises.

5. Don't sit down to work on a first draft of a play unless you can carve out at least two hours of uninterrupted writing time. Like the swimmer jumping into the water, it takes time each time you sit down, to warm up and enter the atmosphere of your play.

6. Don't give up when the going gets tough. Know the difference between an idea that doesn't work as a play, and an idea that fails to capture your imagination, in contrast to a play that has tough problems to be solved. Most of these problems require protracted thinking and mulling, and traveling up paths that go nowhere, only to turn around, go back to the beginning, and take another path or three.

7. Don't write a play that will take more than two and one half hours to perform. (Try, in fact, to keep it to two hours.) The audience does not want to sit there for more than two hours, unless you are Shakespeare. I understand that some contemporary playwrights do write three-hour plays that get produced. However, it has been my experience that most three-hour plays could have used some editing. The playwrights usually direct these plays themselves or have a director who does not dare to assert the need for editing.

8. Don't start writing if you already know everything about your play. Most playwrights succeed because they are writing to ask questions and find possible answers.

9. Don't write without passion, anger, or intellectual curiosity.
10. Don't write a play whose story you cannot articulate.

Exercises in Do's and Don'ts

1. Identify a play that you recognize as a "good" play, but one you would not want to write yourself. Why?

2. Identify three of your plays, whether a ten-minute plays, a one act, or a full-length play. Which of these plays would you be willing to exchange with a contemporary playwright? You give that playwright your three plays and they give you theirs. If there are any of your plays you do not want to give away, state the reasons. This will tell you what you love about that play. That will identify the passion.

3. Write a short scene without a conflict. Then see how boring it is.
    Stage the following scene in two ways:
    A. A woman waits in the waiting room of a train station. She is reading a book. A young man sits down beside her and tries to "pick her up." She is lonely, unattached, and happy for the attention.
    B. A woman waits in the waiting room of a train station. She is reading a book. A young man sits down beside her and tries to "pick her up." She is engaged, waiting for her fiancé, and they are on their way to meet his parents for the first time.

You will quickly see that scene A may be charming, but it has no conflict and will go on and on and on. Both the young woman and the young man want the same thing. In scene B, because of the conflict, their actions differ. The young man tries to get the young woman, and the young woman tries to get rid of the young man. In all probability, one of them is eventually going to leave the scene.

13
CRITICS

No one is more maligned in the theater than the theater critic, unless it is the playwrights themselves. The *New York Times* has the reputation that a review of a drama opening in New York in its pages can make or break the life of that play and playwright. This is true. For as long as I can remember, there has not been a reviewer for that newspaper who hasn't been both feared by the playwriting community and unanimously disliked and distrusted because the critic is judging, as well as influencing, the future of the play.

There are those who claim they never read reviews, and if so, they are spared the joys and sorrows heaped on playwrights by critics. It is also popular, in playwriting circles, to say that if you believe your good reviews, you also have to believe the bad ones. There are also those playwrights who pray for specific critics to review their shows, because they believe they are in good favor with that critic, based on previous reviews, or the opposite — the belief that a critic doesn't understand your work and is likely to decimate it every time they are allowed to review one of your shows.

Some playwrights try to follow patterns in a reviewer's work. This is as close as any of us ever gets to complex mathematical theory. One can add up the number of plays a certain critic liked according to gender, race, sexual preference, and subject matter, and try to calculate some kind of meaningful configuration. For example, it would be of interest to note how many plays that take place in a kitchen were called "domestic" by any one critic, or how many realistic plays were panned. Personally I don't indulge in this, but I was never good at mathematics.

My critic of choice is Elliot Norton, who reviewed for many years for the *Boston Herald American* and the *Boston Globe*. He was known as the Dean of American drama critics. A Harvard-educated man, with the distinctive qualities of a Boston Brahmin, Beacon Hill bred, he was tall, with a shock of white hair, and a stern, but gentle manner. His criticism was always wise and constructive without being patronizing, and without pandering to any kind of current tastes. Playwrights would read his column in an attempt to rewrite their plays, to discover where the problems were. Mr. Norton was incisive and insightful, and usually pretty accurate. He always allowed playwrights to retain their dignity, as well as their respect for the criticism itself. I suppose it was because he didn't have the kind of ego that pondered over the cleverness of his own language. He only cared about one thing — the American theater.

I was fortunate to have him as my first playwriting teacher. At the time, he was teaching at Boston University and took me on, informally and generously, after hearing my first attempt at a musical revue. Under his tutelage I wrote my first real play, *Rousing Up the Rats Again*, about the Holocaust. When I handed him the completed full-length play in two months, he just shook his head. It was too soon. He was the one who advised keeping a play like a child, until it was ready to go out into the world. It was that play which gained me entrance into the Brandeis University MFA program.

While at Brandeis, a series of my one-act plays were produced and reviewed by Elliot Norton in the *Boston Globe*. I remember his review cited the play's strengths and the places where it could use shoring up. It was from Elliot Norton that I learned the gentle art of constructive criticism, in other words, useful criticism. After the productions were over, I met him at a theater production in Boston, and at intermission he told me: "And one final word, the minute you finish one play, get it out and start the next one and never, never stop." I have tried to take that critical advice.

Playwrights remember fragments of mixed, good, and rave reviews of their work — if they read them. But, there is not one among us who cannot recite line for line the worst reviews our work has ever received. For some reason, they stick to our innards.

In going over my papers in preparation for writing this book, I came across a letter I once wrote to the drama critic of the *New York Times* Connecticut Section in August 1982. It was in response to his review of my play *The Desert* and its production at the Sharon Playhouse in Connecticut. The letter reads as follows:

August 15, 1982

To the Drama Critic of the Connecticut *New York Times*:

Dear Critic:

In regards to your recent review of my play *The Desert* in the Connecticut *New York Times*, I am offended by your callousness. Certainly you must think those of us developing playwrights who *do* have the courage to hang in there, open up to your review on a Sunday morning without feeling, without friends and family and colleagues to read "The Desert Is A Dud." There are many playwrights who claim "Oh I never read those reviews," but I do, because maybe there's something to be learned from them. I am sorry you failed to understand my play.

I found your review destructive, insulting, and without grace. Certainly, a play that has been viewed as contemporary and thoughtful, and was considered good enough to win an NEA, couldn't be without redeeming qualities.

Though I do try not to take these things too personally, I am human, and you managed to hurt both my family and me deeply by your non-constructive insults.

Having survived, however, I am back at my desk writing. Please do not come to review one of my plays again.

Yours truly,

Janet Neipris

I never sent the letter, but kept it for years in my desk in a sealed envelope.

The Desert was first produced by Pittsburgh Public Theatre in 1980, then produced by the Sharon Playhouse, Connecticut, in 1982, and then produced in New York in 1985 by the Manhattan Punch Line Theatre, a theater devoted to comedy. The play received strong reviews in New York and went on to be published in a collection of plays by Broadway Play Publishing in 1999.

Exercise in Criticism

Attend three play performances and write a critique of each that is constructive, applauding its strengths and asking some questions that might help the playwright in looking at his or her own work. Write a critique that is both supportive and honest at the same time.

14

THE EDUCATION OF A PLAYWRIGHT

I am convinced that anyone can be a great writer if he can only have the incredible courage to tell the naked truth about himself and other people. That a little technique with words and the willingness to bare heart, soul, and body are really all it takes. But few people know the truth, and fewer have the artistic intent and courage to tell it.

— **Clive Barnes, eminent former drama critic for the** *New York Times*

The passion and courage to see and tell the truth of a story are only the beginning. T. S. Eliot, in his essay "Tradition and the Individual Talent," says, "No poet, no artist of any art has his complete meaning alone." Eliot goes on to say that an entire order exists before the new work arrives on the scene. Therefore, the education of writers demands an awareness of all literature and history that precedes the moment the first line is put down on paper. The new has to be bounced against the back wall of tradition and reinvented. To create, after all, means to fill a space where there was once nothing.

A story is told about the Southern writer Flannery O'Connor, who entered the writing department of the University of Iowa and asked to see Professor Paul Engle, the poet. She began to speak so excitedly to him, and in a backwoods Georgia speech, that he could hardly understand her, "Here," he said, handing O'Connor a pad of paper and a pen. "Write down what it is you want." She wrote, "My name is Flannery O'Connor. I am in another department at this university and I am not happy. I am a writer." She didn't say "I want to be a writer," but "I am a writer."

Talent is born, but the craft of writing has to do with the disciplined training and enlightenment of the playwright. The education of both playwrights and screenwriters in the dramatic writing program at New York University's Tisch School of the Arts involves a progressive series of intensive writing workshops, in addition to a sizable liberal arts component, including studies in American, European, Latin, Asian, and African literature courses and required courses in history, philosophy, art history, and language. In addition, there are required courses in production and critical studies.

The teacher, in a writing program, is meant to act as an instructor in craft, a confirming support, and a stimulus, a caller to battle. In a writing workshop, the teacher is like the doctor in an emergency room. The patients arrive, bringing with them a history and a body of work — characters, dialogue, scenes, situations, plots, all of which have their strengths and weaknesses. My task as instructor is to examine each writer's work, determining the individual topography, and then to confirm and encourage the places of promise and to identify problem areas. In a writing workshop we speak about what is working and what is not. It is not construed as criticism, but rather, as a professional observation of the machinery. If that sounds clinical, it is only meant to remove the sting of mistakenly taking criticism of the writing to mean criticism of the self.

It has become clear to me, after writing and teaching for twenty-five years, that the mysterious process of developing a story has mostly to do with the asking of questions. How did she get here? Why did he come? What is it they want from each other? A play, after all, is the writer questioning the universe, attempting to discover reasons.

We, as teachers, often feel as a parent with a child; if only we could have our students just a little longer, we could do it just a little better. What we hope is that each writer will feel the same way about every script; if only we could rewrite it one more time, it would be, perhaps, closer to perfection.

The story about Picasso is that once he had finished a painting and given it away, he would have to be watched carefully. In a gallery, or in the home of a friend who owned one of his paintings, he would quietly excuse himself, pulling out a packet of paints from his pocket, and proceed — just one more stroke.

What we can teach our writers is emotional honesty, courage that their blue or red is a unique blueness or redness, and to have faith in the middle, when there is just the writer alone with vision, language, and no encouragement, other than their iron will, empowered by a passionate belief in the landscape they are burrowing through.

Freud said that the two most important things in life are self-respect and pleasure. I urge my students to respect the instinct that stirred the work and take pleasure in the journey.

During my eighteen years as chair of the Department of Dramatic Writing at New York University's Tisch School of the Arts, I served under two presidents, President John Brademas and President Jay Oliva, and under two deans, Dean David Oppenheim and Dean Mary Schmidt Campbell. These were formative and expansive years for the university, both for the School of the Arts and for our department, undergraduate and graduate. In that time, we trained what were to become some of America's leading young playwrights. Wherever new plays are being produced today, play-wrights we trained are at the forefront.

Because we are located in New York City, we are fortunate to be able to attract some of our leading playwrights as faculty. Over the years they have included Tony Kushner, Tad Mosel, John Guare, Marsha Norman, Arthur Kopit, Tina Howe, Shirley Lauro, Terrence McNally, Alfred Uhry, Wendy Wasserstein, Michael Weller, Paul Selig, Eduardo Machado, Len Jenkin, Richard Wesley, Elizabeth Diggs, Lynne Alvarez, Lonnie Carter, Leslie Lee, Gary Garrison, Mac Wellman, Maria Irene Fornes, Lanford Wilson, David Ives, Neil Bell, David Greenspan and the late Harry Kondoleon, Stuart Browne, and Venable Herndon. In 2004, Doug Wright, our former student and now Pulitzer Prize winner and Tony awardee returned as a guest professor.

Our department was recently renamed through the generosity of two donors and advocates of young playwrights, and is known, since fall of 2003, as the Rita and Burton Goldberg Department of Dramatic Writing. Rita and Burton Goldberg, lovers of theater, called me up one day and said, "We want to help playwrights. Can we come in and give you some money to help playwrights?" I'm surprised I didn't send a helicopter to fetch them. Their visit resulted in the Goldberg scholarships, the Goldberg readings, the Goldberg play contest and production, the Goldberg guest profes-sorships, and the Rita and Burton Goldberg Theatre. One part of the education of the playwright includes finding those people who are willing to give both financial and emotional support to the developing writer.

In a report to the dean of the Tisch School of the Arts in May 1996 I wrote:

> In establishing a vital university department which trains young writers, there are three key elements:

> What is taught — the curriculum.

Who teaches it — the faculty.

Who is learning — the student body.

A department is only as good as its faculty, even with the strongest curriculum. Therefore, I believe in the recruitment of a diverse faculty who are actively working in their fields and have broad based networks in the theater community. In order to keep those faculty, faculty development, both professionally and academically, has to be encouraged and supported. This has meant that when someone has a play in production, one of us will cover the other's classes, but never for a period of more than two weeks. This is what has given us the most professional writing faculty in the country. We are giving the message that you *can* teach and you *can* write, and we will help you find a way. Added to the faculty is a vigorous and innovative curriculum, including, at one time or another, courses in poetry, short fiction writing, myth, politics, and even once, before my time, a required course in tap dancing, supposedly to lessen stress, although some said it was because the current chair was a former dancer. There have also been courses dedicated to individual playwrights, such as Chekhov or Beckett, and, of course, Shakespeare has always had his own one-year course. Both through vigorous recruitment, in addition to word of mouth and high standards of admissions, we have developed a student body that is diverse geographically, ethnically, and economically, and who continue to amaze us with the power, originality, and promise of their work.

In the graduate program, a two-year course of study, the backgrounds of the applicants are as variable as their ultimate professional successes. In addition to the usual theater, film, or English major applicants, we have accepted students with law and medical degrees, journalists and philosophy students, a merchant marine, an ordained minister, a sixty-year-old mother from Appalachia, and a radical from Romania. Each graduate applicant is required to send fifty pages of manuscript — a play, screenplay, and in some rare instances, fiction. Admission is based primarily on the quality of the written work and the promise of the applicant as a dramatic writer in our graduate department. Although we have had an occasional miss over the years, our choices have proven to be on the mark and continue to result in an outstanding class whose discipline, originality, and commitment to writing and to each other have contributed to a remarkably vigorous and compassionate community of writers.

With the extraordinary support of two presidents and two deans who have encouraged artists who are original thinkers and practitioners, we have been able to educate generations of playwrights, who have gone on to distinguish themselves in their fields.

Graduates of our department have gone on to positions and professions we couldn't have dreamed of in our early days. Besides the working writers in theater, film, and television, some graduates have become book and magazine editors and contributors. One writes the horoscope for a monthly woman's magazine (well, it *is* writing). Another is a minister whose dramatic writing experience informs her weekly sermons. Some have gone on to law and entertainment law; others are literary managers of theaters. Some have become executives in film and television. There are theater and film producers, teachers, political speechwriters, comic book scribes, video game designers, and one former student is writing a cookbook for writers. What seems clear is that wherever the written word is used, which is everywhere, our students are there and working.

An education is defined by the *Oxford English Dictionary* as "the process of nourishing, rearing, training; the development of mental powers and growth, and the molding of some aspect of character."[2] What playwrights want, more than anything, is a sense of belonging and of critical advice and support. We have shaped this kind of community in our classrooms, our offices, and along our corridors, both for our students and for our faculty. After twenty-five years of teaching, my heart still leaps with joy when I enter our building and press the elevator button for the seventh floor. As a playwright and an educator, I am home.

This essay originally appeared in Point of View *(1995) and was revised at the Virginia Center for the Creative Arts. It has been slightly revised for inclusion in the book.*

Three Exercises in the Education of a Playwright

1. Make a list of the one hundred plays you think are the most important for any playwright to read.

2. Read six plays on your list you have never read.

3. Draw up the syllabus for a course in playwriting that meets once a week, two to three hours, and presuming your students have not written a full length play before, but have written scenes, short plays, and one-act plays. Take this year's calendar and start the course the second week in September and have it run through the second week in December, with one week free at Thanksgiving. For each week give the title of a short lecture, schedule what work will be read in class, and give an assignment due the following class. Devise the class so that a full-length play is completed, first draft, at the end of the term. You may also schedule conferences, guest speakers, and other special in-class exercises. One half of the play should be due before Thanksgiving with conferences to follow.

15

WHAT THEY TOLD ME: ADVICE ON WRITING AND OTHER VICES

The question of whether playwriting — or any other form of writing, for that matter — can be taught has long been the subject of articles, speeches, and weeklong seminars. As an educator of playwrights for most of my adult life, I am unequivocal about the answer. Neither talent nor passion nor imagination can be taught, but craft can.

The education of a playwright, of necessity, comprises notebooks filled with advice. Some of it may prove useless, or useless until the project it applies to appears on the writer's horizon. And some advice will collect dust and be destined for "his or her collected pieces of paper."

I wondered, however, if I asked friends, colleagues, and present and former students — all professional writers — what had been the single best piece of advice about writing they were ever given, or would give themselves, what that advice would be.

In reading through the answers, I did try to find a common theme. There were the expected admonishments to get dressed every day, although I do know playwrights who never get dressed until they've completed their writing for the day. The suggestion to keep glued to your chair is given in the face of the distractions that call to all of us. But then too, there are the exceptions, like Hemingway, who preferred to write standing up. The call to passion and truth and simplicity and staying true to your vision were all among the answers. After reading all the responses however, one element was clear. For each writer, the most valuable piece of advice is as different for each one of us as our voices and our subjects. My recommendation is to keep your ears open for that advice which sings to *you*.

The following, in alphabetical order by writer, are the answers I received. This is what they told me:

Walter Bernstein, screenwriter: "There are two pieces of valuable advice I really remember, if you can call them advice. The first was from an older writer who said, 'Writing is rewriting.' The second was from an agent when I was first starting out. He said, 'Kid, all you need is a hit.' I'm not sure which is more valuable."

Susan Birkenhead, lyricist: "I was extremely lucky to have Jule Styne as my mentor. Jule had a rather colorful way of expressing himself, but his advice was pure gold. He used to hammer home the notion that the thought might be complex, but it must be expressed simply. 'Simple,' he would say, 'and elegantly done.' Then he would grab my arm, look me in the eye, (not easy since he was about 5'4" and I'm 5'9" and say, 'remember … it only comes at them (the audience) once, so you better make sure they get it.'"

Lee Blessing, playwright: "My favorite playwriting advice came from Edith Oliver. She told me never to start a line of dialogue with the words 'well' or 'look' (as in 'Look, I've had about enough of you'). I've tried to avoid doing that ever since."

Deloss Brown, playwright: "William Maxwell, who was for many years, the editor of the *New Yorker*, came from Lincoln, Illinois, as did my grandparents. They appear, thinly disguised, in his novels. I came to New York from Boston to meet him and he took me to lunch. He didn't like my novella — um, well, not enough to publish it — but when I told him I had a couple of one-acts in mind to write, he said, "write them quickly." And that's always been my idea of how to write a play — get the draft down on paper in a couple of weeks at most."

Kelly Cherry, poet and novelist: "It must become a habit, the habitual way you think."

Kirsten Childs, playwright, composer, lyricist: "Truth and simplicity."

Connie Congdon, playwright: "From the great American painter Dorothea Rockburne:
1. There's always something wrong — accept that fact and move on.
2. All you have is your belief in yourself and the process. This is also all you need."
   "What I tell writers when they study with me: pro-crastination is a very painful and risky way to create the complete focus that makes you write past all your fears and doubts about your ability, the subject matter, etc. When you procrastinate, you are trying to re-create those successful all-nighters you had in high school where you were too freaked out about not making the deadline that you wrote without stopping, staying in the 'zone,' and

produced something that was very good. Writing without stopping or editing is an excellent way to get a first draft, but you can do that without manufacturing this agonizing state of fear that the procrastination cycle provides. Remember that your ideas, plans, images, bits of dialogue, your plot ideas are very important but that all you have, all you really have, is what's on the page. The files in your head are just so much vapor. And once you start writing, you can't control the outcome, just like in life. And this is the miracle and the gift. So just write without stopping, surprise and entertain yourself, and don't worry about anything. A long time ago, I realized that to not have ever written would be intolerable when I got to the end of my life. I realized that I would rather write badly than not write at all, that I was writing to speak, that writing was a necessity for the health of my spirit.

"John Guare carries a small journal that he writes in, in tiny script. He always seems to have it. When I asked him if he was writing dialogue, ideas for plays, musings, notes, he said all of the above and that Henry James said to write every day to keep from editing yourself."

April De Generis, playwright: "The best thing I ever learned was probably Aristotle's idea of discovery and reversal in the poetics."

Liz Diggs, playwright: "Write what you know." "Glue your ass to the chair." From Israel Horowitz: "There's no such thing as writer's block — only the refusal to write."

Mauro Flores, playwright, screenwriter: "As long as you're alive, you'll have material."

Nancy Ford, book writer, lyricist: "There are two short sentences I can think of that were given to me by headwriters when I began writing dialogue for soap operas: 'Don't make the subtext the text' and, 'Play it, don't say it.'"

Tim Fountain, playwright: "It's always a disappointment."

Charles Fuller, playwright:[1] "Read, study, and learn the language — because it is the only tool you have when you are composing the music of the play. Language is the instrument, so learn it, know what to do with it."

Gary Garrison, playwright: "The phrase 'write what you know' makes me crazy!!! I have a visceral reaction to it. I didn't like hearing it twenty-five years ago, when I started this journey, and I still don't like to hear it even now. When you write what you don't know, you're forced to discover-explore-imagine-conjecture-realize-question-research ... to me it's far more creative."

Barbara Greenberg, poet, playwright: On the jacket flap of Maxine Cumin's first book of poetry and it has marked *me* for life ... "I once read something Marianne Moore wrote that marked me for life. 'We must be as clear as our natural reticence allows us to be. I have tried always to do this, both in diction and in intent, to the point of pain.'"

David Grimm, playwright: "Get the check."

Jim Grimsley, novelist and playwright: "When I was writing my first book, Max Steele from UNC-CH told me to get the details exactly right. He said to describe the floorboards of the porch exactly the way they looked in my memory, to make every detail as much as possible come out of my own sense memories from my time living in that house. He said that this kind of verity was the only way to get through such a difficult story. He turned out to be right."

Rinne Groff, playwright: "Suzan-Lori Parks recommended the setting of deadlines: little ones or big ones. Writing a play takes a long time and requires so much self-motivation. It's nice to have goals to meet along the way to help mark your progress and to encourage you to stay on target."

John Guare, playwright: "I abide by the great Georges Feydeau's one rule of playwriting: character A says my life is perfect as long as character B doesn't show up. Knock knock. Enter character B. Another lesson learned: if you're stuck at a certain point in your script, the problem is never the moment where the trouble seems to be, but is five or six pages earlier."

Carol Hall, composer and lyricist: "My favorite quote about writing is Faulkner's 'You must kill your darlings …' meaning, of course, that you cannot ever fall madly in love with your own work … and my other favorite is really on the same idea: Picasso's 'I sell myself nothing!'"

Sheldon Harnick, lyricist: "Giving advice to a writer, I think, is a lot like giving advice to a mother about to give birth. You can talk about the process, but no matter what you say, it's still going to be painful and chaotic, bloody and sweaty (at least metaphorically). Writing is about the joy of creation. Get through the messy part any way you can."

Tina Howe, playwright: "I never studied playwriting so I've always longed for a wise mentor to give me the secrets of the trade. In his absence, I turned to Emily Dickinson for her advice: 'Tell the truth but tell it slant — Success in circuit lies. ...'"

Xuefei Jin, poet and novelist: "In fall 1992 I took a workshop with Aharon Appelfeld at Boston University. One day he said to us that after he had landed in Israel in the late 1940s, he had become a dance instructor. Most of his students then were middle-aged people, many of whom used to be refugees from Europe. In the dance class they complained a lot about fatigue and pain. Then Mr. Appelfeld lowered his voice and said to us, 'from that class I learned how to write.'"

"Puzzled, we looked at one another around the seminar table. Then Mr. Appelfeld said, 'I wanted to write about how heavy their limbs were.'"

Judith Johnson, playwright: "Getting on with it! As Billy Crystal says in *Throw Momma from the Train*, 'a writer writes!'"

Bryony Lavery, playwright: "Embrace the notion of rewriting."

Leslie Lee, playwright and screenwriter: "The best piece of advice: If you want something in your script, put it there. Don't allow nuance, implication and assumption to always determine your message. Advice to others: Have the courage of your convictions. Have an opinion."

Andrea Lepcio, playwright: "I think the best advice I ever got — and I got it from most every professional writer I have

ever encountered — is write every day. It is all too true
that you have to write bad to write good. By writing every
day, I keep my muscle toned, my heart pumping, and my
imagination reaching. I may throw a lot of pages (or bytes)
away — but it ensures that I am present when the gems
are ready to come out."

Kendra Levin, playwright: "Ask the right questions."

Ben Lobato, playwright, filmmaker: "During my freshman
year I was taking Writing 101 with a professor named
Arnold Davidson. Mr. Davidson was a stickler for detail
and I quickly learned that I knew absolutely nothing
about punctuation, yet I wanted to be a writer. One day I
was feeling so frustrated that I went to speak to Professor
Davidson about dropping out. As I entered his office, he
was busy slashing papers with his red pen, 'Excalibur.' As
I spoke, he continued working without looking up. When
I finished, he asked me if I thought Hemingway worried
about punctuation when he wrote. I said, 'I don't know.'
He looked up from his papers, stared straight into my
eyes, and said, 'You just keep writing. Someday someone
will punctuate for you.'"

Victor Lodato, playwright and poet: "I've always loved the following advice, from Natalia Ginzburg:

'I realized that in this vocation there is no "savings." If someone
thinks "That's a fine detail and I don't want to waste it in what
I'm writing at the moment, I've plenty of good material here,
I'll keep it in reserve for another story I'm going to write," that
detail will crystallize inside him and he won't be able to use it.
When someone writes he should throw the best of everything
into it, the best of whatever he possesses and has seen, all the
best things he has accumulated throughout his life.'

Wonderful, no? It's from Natalia Ginzburg's essay "My Vocation" in her lovely collection of essays *The Little Virtues*.

Craig Lucas, playwright: "Don't tell anyone what you're writing about. Don't re-read until you've put some time between you and what you've written. Keep going. Don't leave the desk. Write as close to waking up in the morning as possible. Don't ask anyone's opinion whom you do not trust profoundly, and keep the number of people small. Write for yourself. Fuck all the rules. Never read critics. Start a new play before the last one opens. Work only with great people whose work you are excited about and admire, and then you have only two options with each and every colleague — trust them or fire them."

Emily Mann, playwright and director: "Listen. Really, really listen. And then, as my dear friend Joyce Carol Oates says, write your heart out."

Donald Margulies, playwright: "The most useful pith I can impart is a reminder to young playwrights that the play they're working on need not contain every idea they've ever had. It's important to know when to *stop* rewriting, put a play away, and move on to the next play. I have seen far too many talented people make a career of rewriting the same play instead of moving forward. Plays are always going to be flawed. But it's important to write new plays that present new problems to solve."

Patty Marx, comedy writer (television): "'I'd love to write like Tolstoy,' a movie producer supposedly once said to a screenwriter, 'but I don't have the time.' Non-writers believe that writers turn on their computers (or pick up a pen) and words simply accumulate. It is, of course, much more difficult than that. Before writing as much as a single word, a writer must do the following: clean grout in shower, fold sweaters in drawer, re-fold sweaters, come up with wish list of items from Neiman Marcus catalogue, look online for lyrics of favorite Bob Dylan song, memorize lyrics, find the thingamajig that fell off the whatchamacallit, vacuum inside grill on top of refrigerator, try on all shoes in closet, experiment with parting hair on other side, ponder issue of which cities to include if there is a book tour, buy a lifetime supply of coffee ice-cream bars, lose five pounds. Unfortunately, after you have done all this, you will have no time left for writing."

Terrence McNally, playwright: "I see no 'value' in any sort of a degree for a writer. In fact, no one has ever asked me if I went to college. However, I treasure the education I got at Columbia very, very highly. School is investment in your entire life, not your 'career.' If your primary goal is film and TV, get thee to LA. If it's theater, go to New York."

Hillary Miller, playwright: "The poet Brenda Shaugnessy once told me that the two words no writer should ever put in a poem are: 'shards' and 'pantyhose.' (When I reminded her of this a year later, she had completely forgotten she ever said it.) Also, in a workshop, playwright Ntozake Shange handed me a full-page list of writers (most of which I'd never heard of before in my life) and commanded, 'Start here. You can't let yourself be ignorant.'"

Edith Milton, fiction writer and essayist: "I think the best advice I ever got was from my husband Peter (who is an artist), and it wasn't advice and it wasn't about writing. It was simply the fact that he went up every day to his

studio, and stayed there. Sometimes he managed to get
work done. Sometimes he just stared at the piece he was
working on. Often he erased everything he'd done the day
before. But he spent the day in the studio — even when
he was teaching, he came back from class and went there
immediately. I was always quite good about meeting deadlines — when I had a project, I would work at it assidu-
ously and get it done on time. But then I would just loaf
around until I had the next deadline — so I really never
did any of my own work. After I married Peter I realized
that I would be very bored while he was in the studio
unless I began to follow his example; and so I set myself a scheduled number of hours for writing every day. I
managed to write my doctoral dissertation and two novels
(one, alas, never published) when our children were babies
— poor little things, they were left to the tender mercies
of a baby-sitter so that their mama could complete her
four hours of isolation and contemplation: mostly what
I accomplished was staring out of the window, but, then,
staring out of the window on a regular schedule can lead
to all sorts of things."

Peter Morris, playwright: "This is the advice I wish I'd gotten
back when I started writing: You need to seek out your
contemporaries and make friends with other writers. This
isn't easy: writers tend to be pretty solitary and also pretty
vain (and therefore unwilling to believe that other writers
even exist). But having friends your own age who are also
writers will keep you humble, it will help you to understand what about your own work is most uniquely *yours*.
And most importantly, it will get you out of the apartment from time to time. (Besides, it's worth noting that
in every generation, the best writers always seem to know

each other: Shakespeare knew Marlowe and Ben Jonson, Elizabeth Bishop knew Marianne Moore and Robert Lowell, and so on. There is no such thing as a solitary genius.

Get out there and do it yourself. Stage your own work, organize your own readings, invite your friends. Don't sit around waiting to be discovered (or mailing off a lot of S.A.S.E.s in the hope of getting discovered). The only "discovery" happens laterally — your contemporaries become familiar with your work, you with theirs, and then one day you all wake up and discover that you've arrived.

Remember that you are in this for the long haul. Writing tends to attract a lot of dilettantes, but eventually you will be rewarded by proving that you're serious enough to stick with it for life. (Besides, like any other way of life, writing is not worth succeeding in if it's not worth failing in.)

And finally, you won't feel sane until you're getting paid. This is depressing, but if you don't have the nerve to keep writing until you start making money at it, then you shouldn't be a writer at all."

Marsha Norman, playwright: "Jon Jory said, 'When you're looking for a good subject for a play, go back ten years in your life, to some time when you were really afraid. Because you were scared, you'll remember all the details of the event, whatever it was. And because it's ten years back and you still remember it, it will be important to you somehow, and thus, worth writing about.'"

Lizzie Olesker, playwright: "As a playwright, you need to wear a cloak of arrogance. You can't be too humble (from Tony Kushner, as I remember it ...)

Perhaps, contradictorily:

You can write anything because you know you can throw it out — Maria Irene Fornes. Irene instilled in me the necessity of following the characters — they're the boss, not you. If you try to control them, you will stifle your play. She taught me to find the breath of the character — to listen to it, feel it. To touch their skin. You can't know a character just by listening to her/him. You need a more visual, visceral experience of them.

From Suzan-Lori Parks, via Tony K. — commit to sitting down to write for just one half hour every day. No more, no less. If it's more, great. If not, don't sweat it. Soon, you'll have a play. Also, from Suzan-Lori — see the words from your characters written on the wall across the room. She writes for the people inside her plays. Write from the gut, not from the head.

And from Mac Wellman — lower your IQ. Avoid the swamp of the already known — it's what you don't think you know that's interesting.

And my own advice (with three kids):

(Very literal, not so interesting perhaps, but bottom line.)

Get out of the house. Find a place to write that's somewhere else …

More specific to playwriting — Put the impulse for your play on a little piece of paper — often for me it's a visual image. Tape it to the wall where you're typing up your play. Look at it every now and then.

Plays are like music — write the score.

Focus on the work itself."

Liz Poliner, poet and novelist: "The single most important advice I ever received is that it is okay to want to write."

Charles Purpura, screenwriter: "If it ain't on the page, it ain't on the stage." "Dying is easy, writing is hard."

Mark Ravenhill, playwright: "Don't be afraid of imitation."

Richard Rhodes, novelist, biographer, and essayist: "Years ago, I came off active duty in the United States Air Force with a pregnant wife and one hundred dollars to my name. I was living in Kansas City at the time and found work at Hallmark Cards, writing the daily employee newspaper. A poet who made his living teaching English told me scornfully that such writing was drivel and I'd be better off driving a cab. But five mornings a week by 10 a.m. I had to fill two sides of an 8 1/2-by-11 sheet of paper with news — of promotions and retirements, of corporate do-ings, of births and marriages and deaths. The forms of the stories I wrote were highly stylized, the contents carefully censored, but every morning by 10 a.m. I had to get the Spam to the front line. At Yale I had chosen not to take the only creative writing course the university offered, which was called Daily Themes and which required a page of original writing delivered to the instructor's door every morning, five days a week. Now Hallmark was paying me to double that production. (The poet would say there's no comparison. He'd be wrong. Every form you learn to write, no matter how mundane, is another tool in your kit.) I worked in the Hallmark public relations department for a man named Conrad Knickerbocker, who had already begun publishing book reviews and fiction. After I got to know Knick a little, I asked him timidly how you become a writer. He said, 'Rhodes, you apply ass to chair.' I call that solid-gold advice the Knickerbocker Rule."[2]

Brooks Robards, poet: "The best writing advice (more than once) I've had is to keep writing (Scribble, scribble, scribble!). And the best one I can give (echoing Hemingway, I think) is write about what you know."

Charles Rubin, television writer: "When I was a freshman at college I drove across Massachusetts to hear William Alfred lecture at Harvard. He was the author of *Hogan's Goat* and, at the time, a long-running famous professor in a huge lecture hall you could slip into unnoticed. Somewhere in the middle of his talk on *Beowulf* he went off-book to describe a lecture by William Faulkner that Alfred had himself attended as a Harvard Ph.D. candidate in the very early fifties. Faulkner was taking questions from the floor when some very earnest stammering kid rose to his feet to say, 'Mr. Faulkner. I intend to be a writer. I have a good deal to say. But can you give me any advice?' to which Faulkner apparently leaned confidentially across the podium at the kid, as if they were the only two in the room, and said, 'Sonnnnn, don't tell any lies.'

These days I have students of my own, and there is always an occasion every semester for me to pass down this story from the Faulkner lecture, to the Alfred lecture, to my own class. I always put it this way: 'Here's something William Faulkner told me. ...'"

Stephen Schwartz, composer and lyricist: "I think every writer, particularly when he or she is starting out, experiences the fear that his or her project will fail, or worse yet, be ignored or never even heard or seen. (This feeling often alternates with the over-aggrandizing feeling that he or she is writing the greatest masterpiece of all time, and one's mood swings back and forth.) This simply comes with the territory.

But if you're going to be a professional writer, that's one of the things you have to deal with. With experience, one's expectations and fears both get more realistic. But I can't tell you that those feelings ever leave entirely.

The best advice I can give you is to try to stay true to your own taste and vision, so that at the end of the day, at least *you* like what you've done."

Lorenzo Semple, Jr., screenwriter: "If you are engaged to rewrite a script, make *sure* that it wasn't secretly written by the producer under a pseudonym. Also, if you have given up smoking, it is helpful to chew on a plastic pen."

Jeff Sweet, playwright: "Cultivate relationships with developing, hungry, talented directors. Attend readings, workshops and showcases to spot rising talents and then invite them out for coffee (or whatever beverage appropriate). Many more productions of my stuff have happened because directors have been passionate advocates of my scripts than because of agents' submissions. Good directors can often walk right past a theater's literary manager and pitch a project directly to the artistic director."

Alred Uhry, playwright: "Frank Loesser told me I had to be able to defend every syllable I wrote. I was, I think, 22. I've tried never to forget that."

Ed Valentine, playwright: "Get out of the house. Get out of the house for writing of course, especially if you don't have a home office, try writing at the library, the coffee shop, or the back pew of the church. It's more than that, though. This advice means: get out of the house to live. So when I feel stuck, I close the journal, leave the pen at home, and I get out of the house to visit: art museums, arboretums, zoos, freak shows, carnivals, clam bars, concert halls, cock-tail lounges, 4-H fairs, obscure historical sites, abandoned roadside attractions, and of course: beaches, both empty and full. None of these places are really for research, and most of them aren't conducive to writing (though writing will surely arise) but all them feed hungers, douse me with images, and send me home with something to write about, guaranteed."

Richard Walter, screenwriter: "Real writers hate writing; we love *having written*."

"Tommy Thompson was asked what single piece of advice he could give writers, if he could give just one. He said, 'Everyday, no matter what else you do, get dressed.'"

Wendy Wasserstein, playwright: "The best advice I ever got about playwriting was from Lloyd Richards. He told me about *uncommon women*: 'your characters can be ambigu-ous but *you* can't be ambiguous. It may seem clumsy to you but somewhere the audience needs to know your point of view.'"

Mary Lou Weisman, essayist, nonfiction writer: "Figure on at least ten drafts.
    Another good piece of advice comes directly from William Strunk and E. B. White's *Elements of Style*: 'Vigorous writing is concise. A sentence should contain no unnecessary words, a paragraph no unnecessary sentences. For the same reason that a drawing should have no un-necessary lines and a machine no unnecessary parts. This requires not that the writer make all the sentences short, or avoid all detail and treat subjects only in outline, but that every word tell.'

Richard Wesley, playwright and screenwriter: "When I was a freshman at Howard University, the chair of the drama department, Owen Dodson, upon hearing of my teenaged disappointment at learning that the department was not teaching screenwriting, leaned forward in his chair as I sat in his office, fixed me with a determined stare and said forcefully, 'Child, if I can teach you to write for theater, you will be able to write for anything.'"

Doug Wright, playwright and screenwriter:[3] "People say to write what you know, but I always say to write what you don't know. Write what vexes and confuses and infuriates you."

"Narrative is primary. We still go to the theater to hear bedtime tales. Storytelling is one of the first ways that parents impart knowledge to their children."

Maury Yeston, lyricist: "I think it essential, for young writers just starting out, to never avoid the obvious — what is obvious to you may well be non-obvious to the rest of the world."

Exercise in What They Told Me

1. List five of the most important things you've ever been told about playwriting.

2. List five central things you would tell a student of playwriting.

16
TO BE A PLAYWRIGHT

When Hamlet questions his life in the famous soliloquy, Act III, Scene 1, there is the question of whether to go on, whether to continue suffering the slings and arrows of outrageous fortune or not. In Shakespeare's play, it is a moment marked by choice. When we, as writers, are at those same crossroads and decide in favor of life — the life of a playwright — part of our success, emotionally and professionally, depends on our understanding the rules of the contract we're making. If we are signing on for the long run, we are agreeing to "bear those ills we have," as playwrights, those "outrageous fortunes," rather than turning to more certain professions, like those of mathematicians, physicists, or accountants, where the square root of 625 is forever 25, and don't ask me why. I have it on authority from my husband who is an engineer.

Recently, while working in England, I was at a meeting of a group of playwrights from the National Theatre. They ranged in age from the youngest, Judith Johnson and Philip Riddley, to the more established Patrick Marber, to the old guard, the not-so-old and quite vibrant Snoo Wilson. Though differing widely in styles and subjects, there was a striking common denominator. They all expressed a very private and unsolicited gratitude to be playwrights in this world. They felt it was an honor and privilege to work at what you truly wanted to do, and to work, especially, in the aliveness, the vibrancy of theatre.

Previous generations, both here and abroad, have traditionally been beset by financial necessity and societal conformity and confirmation. Who would want their child to be a writer, beleaguered by uncertainty, rejection, and probable economic hardships? Who would choose, for anyone, days of isolation, nights of terror, and months of work, which might wind up in a wastebasket?

And what about the plethora of inevitable carrots held out in the theatre — "They are reading it" (which could mean the intern is reading it, and if you teach, it could even be one of your students), or the more heartening "it's under consideration," which could mean no one has read it yet, or they can't find it, or indeed they've read it, and it is in a towering pile of "maybes," to the highly encouraging "we like it and we'd like to hold on to it" and you are wondering what that means. Hold it close to you? Put it on hold? Hold it for how long? Or, someone tells you "Perhaps we will do a workshop." No, no, not "do," but "consider." "Yes, a possible workshop," until it's finally "No" either because the theatre is thoughtful enough to tell you so or fails to contact you at all or, even worse, you receive next season's schedule in the mail and your name isn't there.

We are always trying to interpret the rhetoric. I remember early on being told by a film producer that he had read my script and had decided to "pass on it." I was deliriously happy. They were going to pass it on to someone else to read. That was a good sign. Oh how wrong! I later learned what "pass" meant. You were being passed by. It was a euphemism for "We don't want you." In the theatre there are different covered meanings. "No" is often "It does not fit our season." You are out of season.

Or, yet another scenario; the play is to be produced, but always lurking there, once produced, is the distinct possibility of public embarrassment, by critics and audience alike. So, you see why, historically, few parents of practical and sane minds have ever urged their offspring to go out and write for the not-for-profit theatre.

Is it an honor to work in the theatre? Is it more of an honor in England? An American colleague suggested it is because the theatre, film, and television industries in Britain are all located in one city, London. This eliminates the choices demanded of American writers, directors, and actors of living in either Hollywood or New York. The ability to more easily earn a living wage as a playwright by writing across all the mediums, just by walking a few blocks, certainly ensures a modicum of income and dignity.

In this country, however, we lack adequate government subsidization of the theatre and all arts. Also, we can't easily move the city of Los Angeles to New York. We can, however, wage a continuing fight for added government and corporate financial support of the arts.

Yet, still, we have something important to learn from our British counterparts. We have all chosen to be playwrights. For most of us, this is the realization of a dream, and for some, a dream we didn't even know we had when we were young. Joan Didion says in her book of essays *Slouching Towards Bethlehem*, that self respect means understanding the price of things, the price of our choices.[1]

Every day, as a playwright, I am conscious I've chosen terror, uncertainty, confusion, isolation, and the possibility of absolute rejection and devastating humiliation, but I am what I want to be in this world, and that is no small thing. You bet it is an honor and privilege to be a dramatist. To be honorable, after all, means to stand upright, to have principles, to have a moral code; and to be privileged implies you have opportunity and freedom. Don't we?

So, what, ultimately, does it mean to be a playwright? What is the price? What is our bargain with the devil? What is our payoff? And what, finally, is our morality?

The price, for one thing, is the certainty of the possibility of failure. Understand that. Let it never be a surprise to you. Then what is the payoff? Well with assuredness, as a playwright, you can count on your choice of subject and preferred process. You are in complete control. You're the boss. No one cares how or when you get the job done. If, on the other hand, you want to work for someone else, hurry and sign on and report to an 8 to 5 government job; but don't forget to punch the timeclock every day.

But that's not what you've chosen. You can sleep all morning or never, or you can be one of those writers, in our long tradition, who frequent cafés after their day's work, from SoHo to San Francisco to Paris, and all the Starbucks in between.

My husband, who worked for the government as an engineer for many years, used to ask me who those people were who were sitting in the cafés near our home in Greenwich Village. Didn't they have jobs? Well they did, but they kept their own odd but accountable hours. Now that he's a full-time sculptor, he understands. We artists have freedom of choice, and for that, we must keep our bargains and willingly pay the price or get out.

What else can we count on as playwrights? We can be assured the very act of creation. Architects have it, painters, weavers, composers, scientists, and designers — all making something where there was formerly thin air, where nothing existed.

What more is assured? Clearly, if you complete your work, if you pile up the pages, if you finally reach that page where you type in "the end," it's certain you will experience a swelling feeling of accomplishment. By swelling, I don't mean a swelled head, but a kind of rising, a gradual lifting up, an enlargement of what you started with — a phrase, a picture, or a buried vision.

I love to hold all the pages of a student's completed script in my palm, weigh the work in, feel the completeness of it in my hands. And, completion, as a playwright, is so within your grasp. Not every profession has that possibility. The engineer who does the calculations for the new bridge never accomplishes the entire bridge, nor does the worker on the assembly line for everything from automobiles to cardboard boxes have the satisfaction of the achievement of the whole. You are that thing that so many people want to be — a writer, from beginning to middle to end. It's all yours.

Why the universal romance with the idea of being a playwright? Our dentists envy us, our barbers think our lives are glamorous, our accountants don't exactly get it after they do our taxes, but it all sounds terribly exciting. I believe what others see is our freedom and our openness to all things, including the possibility of ecstasy. This is what makes what we do so desirable. If it's so to others, can it be the same truth for us? Can we be cognizant of our freedom?

Once, I asked a Buddhist where joy came from. He answered without hesitation that it came from an openness to life. If the price of being a playwright is the certain possibility of failure, and the payoff is our assured freedom and consequent intermittent moments of joy, then what is our morality? Is it individual or collective?

As a group, I think we do have a responsibility to be truth tellers, and soul searchers. As artists we are inner-directed. We are not about how we look, but about how we are. We are in direct opposition to that part of our current society which is outer directed, from Ugg boots to the armored Hummers some people are driving around in. As writers we're asking, "How am I being?" rather than "How am I looking?" Our collective morality is as questioners of our universe.

Probably the strongest individual moral imperative we all can have is Joseph Campbell's urging to follow our bliss. A visual artist I respect and admire for both his work and his work ethic claims that morality ruins art, and it is only passion that lifts it.

Norman O. Brown in his book *Life Against Death* says that the highest form of art is when work becomes play. My same artist friend tells me he rarely goes on vacation and that he is happy only when he's in his studio working. He says for him, it is as though he is still a little boy in his room behind a closed door, building model airplanes. Perhaps that thrill is what we all want to capture. Like airplanes coming in for a landing, we all come at that ecstasy of spirituality, that morality, from different directions. Some seldom leave the ground or the room where they write, others circle the skies before landing in front of the computer, and still others have dangerous forced landings — we get so tired of procrastination, of giving our identities as playwrights when we know we aren't writing, that out of total loss of self-respect, finally, with no place to turn, we land and turn to the work at hand.

I once read that the definition of insanity is to repeat the same actions and expect different results. So many playwrights I know have difficulty getting to their desks, when that is the one thing, experientially, that will give them pleasure. Why the difficulty in getting down to work? Is it the prospect of failure? Or is it the probability we have no idea what we're doing, or have nothing to say? In fact, we are completely and hopelessly confused and seemingly lost. But we already said that was part of the contract, the expected, much the same as a contractor can expect to hit dirt and rocks and water when building a house. And we all know we only find out what it is we are writing about by writing.

So why would we repeatedly repeat the action of avoiding our desks?

It's true, once playwrights begin to work, they feel better, they feel they are home, they feel the possibility of the whole. Because at work, in the struggle with character and language, with focus and message, the writer is doing what he or she was meant to do.

So our morality is, in a way, based on our passion, and that passion is synonymous with truth, and truth means being true to your individual voice — what you see and think and feel. Every time we follow our instincts as playwrights, rather than what we decide would be commercially viable, we are being faithful to what characterizes our voice and style as writers, what differentiates one from the other. Originality is never cerebrally conceived, but rather stems from something deep inside that we dare to follow.

To be a playwright is to head into the sun, is to expand every day rather than retract. It is work that has its origins with us, and therein is original, work that is audacious, which connects, which either breaks the heart or celebrates it. We are always heading into the sun.

The playwright is often holding a light up to the cracks in people's lives, showing where the everyday bleeds at the heart. When you think of those kinds of moments in fiction or poetry or drama, that make men more human and less alone, then you remember why we are writing. We want to create our own moments that illuminate the fissures. And that is because the greatest distance we know is between any two individuals, and we, as writers for a living theatre, have to breach that abyss.

In William Maxwell's short novel *So Long, See You Tomorrow*, there is a section at the beginning where a young boy is brought out of his room to meet his new stepmother, shortly after his own mother's death. The hero, in describing the moment, says how he longs to go back through the door to where it was still the time before his mother died, but that door has closed behind him. He can't go back into that room. Raymond Carver, in his short stories, focuses on characters who, at the moment they realize that things will be the same forever, are faced with an event that ensures the realization that they will never be the same again.

In Thornton Wilder's *Our Town* — incidentally voted the favorite play of Dramatists Guild members when polled a few years ago — there is the scene where Emily, now dead, elects to go back and watch one day in her life and is decimated by our lack of attention to one another, or that moment in *The Glass Menagerie* when Amanda learns that the gentleman suitor for Laura, after all her fixings, is not available. Hope is dashed and we're left bleeding on the sidewalk with Amanda and Laura. These are the moments that show us our faces and the cracks in our souls.

I will never forget the scene in Neil Simon's *Plaza Suite* when the hero, played by George C. Scott in the performance I saw at Circle in the Square in New York, is at the Plaza celebrating an anniversary with his wife, played by Maureen Stapleton. He is despondent and his wife says she doesn't understand it. He has everything he always wanted — a fine position, a wonderful family, a beautiful home, travel ... "What is it you want?" Scott takes a deep breath, then his powerful face turns all soft and quiet and he says in almost a whisper, this powerful giant of a man, "I just want to do it all over again.... I would like to start the whole damned thing right from the beginning."[2] It is one of the best moments in theatre, one of longing and loss, and the reason why every playwright from Euripides to Chekhov to Williams and O'Neill and Albee in *Who's Afraid of Virginia Woolf* to Kushner in *Caroline, or Change* is searching with his own flashlight for the same such moment — the one where the we bleed at the heart.

Martha, near the end of Albee's play, *Who's Afraid of Virginia Woolf*, pleads with her husband to have her fantasy reinstated, the rebirth of their imaginary son, "You didn't have to kill him," she cries, and he only answers, without emotion, "Requiescat in pace."

Or in Tony Kushner's *Caroline, or Change*, there is the acknowledgment of the gulf between the black maid Caroline and young Noah, played out in the catacombs of hell, the basement laundry, in a play which puts Caroline in a future beyond the possibility of any dreams or change.

When I was a young woman, an undergraduate at Tufts University in Medford, Massachusetts, just outside of Boston, it came to me to introduce Robert Frost who would be reading at our chapel that evening. I heard him in that gravelly voice read his poem "The Oven Bird." "The song the bird doth sing," Frost said, "is what to make of a diminished thing."3

As a playwright I have been asking that question ever since — all the lost dreams, expectation ground to ashes. Arthur Miller said that tragedy arises when we are in the company of a man who has missed accomplishing his joy — but the joy must always be possible, just within his reach. That's what makes it tragic, what breaks our hearts in the theatre.

Also, in drama, there is the celebration of the struggle. Sometimes what is won is not always the thing the character went after, but something other. People just miss their targets. The timing is off. It comes, but it comes too late. We are always looking in front of our right shoulder, but what we want often arrives from behind the left shoulder. And that is what gives both us, and our characters, hope — that thing that keeps us going.

I love the indomitability of the human spirit, how you can't keep us down, how when the slings and arrows hit us, all we can do is roll up our sleeves and go straight through the middle, no short cuts.

To be a playwright means, more than anything, we care about people and how they got to be the way they are. We understand what is "characteristic" of them, where it comes from and where it takes them. We recognize what they say — the spoken dialogue — and imagine what they're thinking or feeling, the subtext, at the same time, and with the two, we try to decipher the truth.

Since the Greek derivation of the word "drama" is action, we agree that our characters are defined only by their actions. These actions, one leading to the other in linear plays or in a controlled "shattered glass" nonlinear play, pieced together and adding up to the sum, both constitute plot. Plot is what happens to our characters as opposed to situation, which marks where a play starts.

The first argument over plot I ever had was with a beginning film writer. His thankfully short script had a clothes drier going round and round, and the camera on a close-up of this activity. Fifteen minutes of this. When I pointed out nothing was changing, he disagreed — the laundry was getting drier. But his main argument was that the script was supposed to be boring because it simulated the boredom of life. Case stated. If you *are* characterizing a bore in drama, it had better be the most fascinating bore ever, and likewise with a scene.

Being a playwright is predicated on your ability to practice serious working habits. We all know it. Why would we practice less than serious habits? In addition, we have to know where to find our stories and, more importantly, to be able to read our own hearts. The stories we write have to stir our juices — our anger and fury and passion. Then, will the story sustain? Then, how will we tell this story? And what questions will you ask in the crafting of the play — questions of location and character arcs, motivation and tone, inciting and dramatic incidents, and climaxes of no return and those of realization. In chapter 3 are listed fifty questions a playwright can ask when writing a play. We create by asking ourselves these questions. If we knew the answers, most of us would have no reason to write.

Recently, I visited an old friend, a very talented artist who had tired of painting. So she had stopped. She claimed all she was doing was accumulating product. She did sell, but not enough to keep up with her productivity. "Why paint more?" she asked, "and for whom? I don't need it for my ego," she told me. When I shared that I was working harder than I ever had, and sometimes was exhausted, she advised me to cut way back on work, pointing out that I should be able to put that ego trip aside.

I thought about it, but I was certain it was no ego trip. Then she asked me why I wrote. I told her there were just all these things I wanted to do — a new children's musical, and the play about South Africa, and the book I was writing, and then there was this other play I was thinking about. I was writing because I wanted to, because I was passionate about working on these projects.

Later I thought about my friend. Was she simply burnt out or depressed? I concluded it was neither of these, but that she had lost one thing — desire, and without that, the artist is dead.

The writer in us stands solitary on the rooftop, arms stretched to the sky, face to the sun, one foot rooted in rules and the other foot set to jump from that roof and fly, free as a bird.

To be a playwright is to be grateful, because we are living the life we've chosen, and because it is an honor and privilege to write for the theater and show audiences their faces and their humanness. To be a playwright means we have the freedom to fly. And that freedom is spectacularly precious.

NOTES

Chapter 1

1. See http://www.brainyquote.com/quotes/quotes/s/
   sigmundfre165464.html.

Chapter 2

1. Virginia Woolf, *A Room of One's Own* (Harcourt, 1929 © 1957
   by Leonard Woolf) p. 69.
2. Nancy Hale, *A Life in the Studio* (Boston: Little, Brown &
   Co., 1957).
3. Lillian Westcott Hale, a celebrated Boston portrait painter
   during the interwar years.

Chapter 4

1. J. Bronowski, *The Identity of Man* (New York: The
   Doubleday/Natural History Press, 1965) p. 95.

Chapter 5

1. George Piece Baker, *Dramatic Technique* (Greenwood, 1970, © 1919 by George Pierce Baker) p. 309.
2. Janet Neipris, *After Marseilles,* © 2005 by Janet Neipris, p. 44
3. Tina Howe, *Painting Churches* from *Coastal Disturbances: Four Plays* (New York: Theatre Communications Group, 1989) p. 145.
4. Lanford Wilson, *The Hot L Baltimore* (New York, Hill and Wang, 1973)
5. Janet Neipris, *Exhibition* © 1975 by Janet Neipris p. 6.
6. Anton Chekhov, *The Cherry Orchard.* Translated by Julius West, 1916. See www.drama21c.net/writers/chekhov/cherryorchard.htm
7. Sam Shepard, Seven Plays (New York: Bantam, 1981). *Curse of the Starving Class,* © 1976 by Sam Shepard, pp. 173–174.
8. David Henry Hwang, *M. Butterfly* (New York: Dramatists Play Sevice, 1988) p. 51
9. Lanford Wilson, *Burn This* (New York: Hill and Wang, 1987) p. 25.

Chapter 6

1. Hippocrates. *Works of Hippocrates.* W. H. S. Jones and E. T. Withington, eds. (Cambridge, Mass.: Harvard University Press, 1923).
2. *Arthur Miller's Collected Plays.* (New York: Viking Press, 1981).
3. Arthur and Barbara Gelb, *O'Neill* (New York: Harper and Row, 1974).
4. Eugene Ionesco, *The Chairs,* Donald M. Allen, trans. (New York: Grove Press, 1958). p. 80.

Chapter 7

1. Editor Lesley Brown, T*he New Shorter Oxford English Dictionary* "Ending," Volume 1 A–M, (Oxford: Clarendon Press, 1993) p. 817

2. Editor George Plimpton, *Playwrights at Work*, "John Guare" (New York: The Paris Review and the Modern Library, 2000) p. 325.

3. Peter Brooks, *Readings for the Plot* (New York: Alfred Knopf, 1984), .

4. Arthur Miller, *The Theatre Essays of Arthur Miller*, "Family in the Modern Drama" (New York: Penguin, 1984) p. 69.

5. Conor McPherson, *Shining City* (London: Nick Hern Books, 2004) pp. 12–13.

6. Ibid., pp. 63–65.

7. Langston Hughes, *The Collected Poems of Langston Hughes*, "Harlem [2]" (New York: Alfred A. Knopf, 1994) p. 238.

8. Lorraine Hansberry, *A Raisin in the Sun* (New York: Random house, 1995) p. 125

9. Ibid., p. 129.

10. Ibid., p. 132.

11. Ibid., p. 135.

12. Wendy Wasserstein, *The Sisters Rosensweig* (Philadelphia: Harcourt Brace, 1994) pp. 107–109.

13. Lyrics to "Shine on Harvest Moon" are by Jack Norworth, © 1918.

14. Anton Chekhov, *The Three Sisters*. Translated by G.R. Ledger © 1998, G.R. Ledger. See http://www.oxquarry.co.uk/threesis.htm.

15. Caryl Churchill, *Far Away* (London: Nick Hern Books, 2000) pp. 36–37.

16. Sam Shepard, *Seven Plays* (New York: Bantam, 1981). *Curse of the Starving Class*, © 1976 by Sam Shepard, p. 198.

17. Ibid., p. 200
18. Editor George Plimpton, *Playwrights at Work* (New York: The Paris Review and the Modern Library, 2000)
19. Susan Letzler Cole, *Playwrights in Rehearsal: the Seduction of Company* (New York: Routledge, 2001).
20. Janet Neipris, *The Bridge at Belharbour* © 1975 by Janet Neipris, p. 35.
21. Ibid., p. 38
22. Ibid., p. 38
23. Janet Neirpis, *After Marseilles* © 2005 by Janet Neirpis, pp. 86–88.

Chapter 8

1. Mary McLaughlin, "Ernest Hemingway, Synonymous with Style: from *Verge Magazine*, February 2001. See http://vergemag.com/0201/features/feat2.html
2. Ibid., source 58.
3. Ibid., source 59.
4. Christopher Rawson, "Scenes from August Wilson" from the *Pittsburgh Post-Gazette*, March 24, 1998. See http://www.post-gazette.com/magazine/19980324bwilson5.asp.
5. Heard, Elizabeth J., "August Wilson on Playwriting: an Interview" from *African American Review*, Volume 35, Spring 2001
6. From Anton Chekhov's letters, August 6, 1891. See http://etext.library.adelaide.edu.au/c/chekhov/anton/c51lt/chap70.html..

Chapter 10

1. A small delegation was written with a Rockefeller
   Fellowship to Bellagio, an NEA grant, and first produced
   under a W. Alton Jones grant. The play opened at the
   Harold Prince Theater, Annenberg Center, Philadelphia,
   in June 1992, and was produced by the Philadelphia
   Festival Theater for New Plays. The cast and creative
   contributors were:
   Remy . . . . Joyce Lynn O'Connor
   Sun . . . . Freda Foh Shen
   Philip . . . . Terry Layman
   Elizabeth . . . . Anne Newhall
   Mei Yen . . . . Tina Chen
   Comrade WU . . . . Mel Duane Gionson
   Sherwood/Passport Officer . . . . Shi-Zheng Chen
   Lili . . . . Bai Ling
2. Clifford A. Reilly, "A Journey Toward New
   Understanding" *Philadelphia Enquirer*, June 1992.
3. Janet Neipris, *Plays by Janet Neipris* (New York, Broadway
   Play Publishing, 2000).
4. Interviews with Contemporary Women Playwrights
   by Kathleen Betsko, Rachel Koenig, Beech Tree Books,
   Simon & Schuster, 1987.
5. A revised script of *A Small Delegation* was produced in
   Beijing by the China Your Arts Theatre, in April 1995,
   trnslated and directed by Shi-Zheng Chen. The cast were
   Remy . . . . Wang Li Yun
   Liu Zin (Sun) . . . . Yang Qing
   Philip . . . . Shi Wei Jian
   Elizabeth . . . . Zhang Ziao Li
   Mei Yen . . . . Zhang Ying
   Comrade Wu . . . . Chen Qiang
   Sherwood Passport Officer . . . . . . Wan Nan
   Lili . . . . Wang Qing Mei

Chapter 11

1. Louis Owens, *The Grapes of Wrath, Trouble in the Promised Land* (Boston: Twayne, 1989).
2. Peter Parnell, "Guild Seminar, The Real Person in Your Play," Moderated by Ralph Sevuch, from *The Dramatist: The Journal of the Dramatists Guild of America* November/ December 2004. pp. 5–10.
3. Jessica Blank and Erik Jensen, "Guild Seminar, The Real Person in Your Play," Moderated by Ralph Sevush, from *The Dramatist: The Journal of the Dramatists Guild of America* November/December 2004. pp. 5–10.
4. Emily Mann, *Still Life: A Documentary* (New York: Theare Communications Group, 1979) p. 70.

Chapter 14

1. T.S. Eliot, "Tradition and the Individual Talent" from *The Sacred Wood: Essays on Poetry and Criticism*, 1922. See http://www.bartleby.com/200/sw4,hml.
2. Editor Lesley Brown, *The New Shorter Oxford English Dictionary* "Education," Volume 1 A–M, (Oxford: Clarendon Press, 1993) p. 785.

Chapter 15

1. Interview with Charles Fuller, *The Dramatist, The Journal of the Dramatists Guild of America, Inc.* (November/ December 2004), p.29.
2. Richard Rhodes, *How to Write* (New York: William Morrow and Company, 1995), pp. 2–3.

3. Interview with Doug Wright, *The Dramatist, The Journal of the Dramatists Guild of America, Inc.* (November/December 2004), pp.13–14.

Chapter 16

1. Joan Didion, *Slouching Towards Bethlehem* (New York: Noonday Press, 1968) p. 145
2. Neil Simon, *Plaza Suite*, from *The Collected Plays of Neil Simon, Volume 1* (New York: Random House, 1971) p. 529.
3. Robert Frost, Mountain Interval, "The Oven Bird" (New York: Henry and Hold Company, 1931). See http://www.bartleby.com/br/119.html.

INDEX

Copyright Page Information

(continued from page iv.)